D0179831

A
Foxy Old Woman's Guide
to Traveling Alone

A
Foxy Old Woman's Guide
to Traveling Alone

Around Town and Around the World

By Jay Ben-Lesser

The Crossing Press
Freedom, CA

Dedicated, with thanks,
to my teachers and mentors—
William Decker • Sandra Scofield • Lawson Inada

Copyright © 1995 by Jay Ben-Lesser
Cover design by Amy Sibiga
Cover photo by Matthew Ben-Lesser
Interior design by Victoria May
Printed in the U.S.A.

Library of Congress Cataloging-in-Publication Data
Ben-Lesser, Jay.
    A foxy old woman's guide to traveling alone : around town and
around the world / Jay Ben-Lesser.
        p. cm.
    Includes index.
    ISBN 0-89594-789-7 (paper)
    1. Travel. 2. Women travelers. I. Title.
G151.B46 1995
910' .24042--dc20   95-30861
                                                              CIP

CONTENTS

INTRODUCTION

With this book I am delighted to share with you some of the knowledge I have acquired traveling alone for nearly thirty years. Whether I was married or single, most of my travels have been alone. My husband never had my lust for travel. He hated our trips together, and I didn't have a good time either. So, after a few unhappy experiences when I insisted that he accompany me, I began to go alone.

I have been around the world thirteen times, lived in Asia and the Middle East for eight years, love Mexico and am in awe of the natural beauty of Canada. I've stayed in some of the world's greatest and most expensive hotels, savoring their comfort and elegance. I've stayed at youth hostels, YMCAs, pensions and bed-and-breakfast inns, and enjoyed the experiences. For twenty years I've traveled and camped in Volkswagen campers. Airlines, trains, buses, cruise ships and sailboats have all caressed me, buffeted me and carried me safely on my adventures. Recently I bought a used motor home, so a whole new world of travel is beginning for me.

I am writing this book for all who dream of traveling but stop themselves. If you really want to travel, you can. You can start right now.

I'll take you through every step you need to become a happy and successful independent traveler. Whether you want to travel around the world or stay closer to home, this book will teach you how to get the most value for the time, energy and money you spend.

I hope you are ready to concentrate on your own personal dreams and expect to make them come true. Now, take responsibility for fulfilling your dreams of travel. This book is for you.

I emphasize low- to medium-budget travel because I think it's the most interesting way to go, plus it extends your adventures by saving money. Even if you have unlimited financial resources, you'll find details in this book to encourage and enrich your travels.

Curiosity and respectful interest in the planet and its people are the characteristics necessary for becoming a good traveler, not the amount of formal education you've completed or how many times you've been around the world.

Part One is intended especially for the shy, inexperienced single woman who wants to travel solo, as well as for the married woman who has never traveled alone. Divorce or death of a partner often leave an experienced traveler immobilized. Years of travel as part of a couple may even be a handicap. If you want to start moving again, here's how—step-by-step. You'll begin with library research, then start going out on your own to movies and restaurants. You'll soon move on to day trips, overnights and extended journeys. You'll quickly discover the special freedom traveling on your own can give you. Most importantly, Part One teaches you how to enrich your life by improving the use of your senses through specific awareness exercises.

In Part Two you'll take advantage of all the learning experiences of Part One and move into the nitty-gritty of traveling alone. In this section I give my personal tips on clothes, luggage, personal safety and the safety of your valuables. Also included is information about obtaining a passport, locating budget sleeping accommodations such as youth hostels and the "Y," camping, and how to choose a cruise. Other topics covered here are invitations from men, working while traveling and traveling with children (after you become an experienced solo traveler). Along the way I share my special tricks for lively travel.

In the Epilogue, I "put it all together" by describing for you how I spent seven exhilarating days in New York City.

I suggest that you read Part One slowly, follow the awareness exercises and risk the experiences. Then go on to Part Two. Or pick a topic that interests you and follow your interests throughout the book. If you choose not to do the awareness exercises, you'll miss much of the value of this book. Experienced travelers who follow and practice the awareness exercises will find that their everyday lives and travel become brighter, clearer, and more colorful. Sensational living and traveling are the rewards.

Finally, I'd like to say a few words about my own thoughts and prejudices concerning travel:

Excitement/anxiety: These twins pull us toward new experiences—and stop us at the threshold. The anticipation of pleasure, stimulation, amusement, and new knowledge is the excitement of travel. Expectations of pain, frustration, trouble, and panic all reflect the anxiety of travel. The physiology of these two emotions is very similar. Dry mouth, sweaty palms, shortness of breath and racing heartbeat are all part of our fight-or-flight survival mechanism.

When we are anxious, we are mentally trying to deal with an imagined future experience. If we breathe deeply and open all our senses to the present, we can *do* something in the present. We are competent people, and the same competence that has kept us alive thus far needs to be with us when we travel.

Tourist: A vacationer. This person is primarily going *away* from somewhere or something. It's good to get away from our hectic and often unsatisfying everyday lives. However, this book is mostly about going *toward* a richer life experience through travel. To be a tourist and to be a traveler are not the same thing, even though they may look the same in a crowd. If you listen, the tourist will probably be talking about the great meal she had in another country last year as she absentmindedly eats a ham sandwich on white bread. The traveler will be looking closely at the regional food she has ordered and perhaps asking the waiter how it was prepared.

Traveler: One who goes forth into the world to explore, to venture, to experience, to learn, to see, to hear, to taste, to smell and to touch. To discover how life is lived in other places and cultures. A traveler wants to become broadly acquainted with life on this planet, as well as with the planet itself. *A traveler wants to return home changed in some profound way.*

Enthusiasm: (from the Greek en theos, "in God"). The God within us must be present in our yearning for travel. Passion, vigor, elan, spunk, verve, vitality, zest, delight, diligence and zeal will carry us through the most exhausting, frightening or ecstatic travels. Travel both feeds and is fed by enthusiasm.

Curiosity: Curiosity is the mother of finding our relatedness to our world. The traveler is drawn to unknown peoples, places and things by her interest in unexpected, unusual, exotic or simply different ways of being in the world. She may derive pleasure and reassurance from the similarity between herself and other peoples. Without curiosity we are doomed to isolation and poverty of experience.

Lust for travel: Travel is not for everyone. If you have hunger, yearning, desire, craving, appetite or simply an urge to travel, do it. However, if your interest in travel is motivated by "I *should* travel," don't bother. Traveling can be hard work, requiring time and energy perhaps better spent on the realization of some other desire. If you have a lust for travel, read on. Come with me, and I will lead you to the land of your dreams.

PART ONE

Nine Steps to
Confident Solo Travel

"The woman who travels alone can start today; but the one who travels with another must wait until the other is ready."

—Henry David Thoreau

Traveling is more than movement through physical space. To travel is to explore new behaviors, to discover the world with new awareness and stimulate a fresh experience of oneself.

Do you feel okay eating out alone? Do you go to movies on your own? All of us have been afraid to go to public places alone. The world is set up for couples and does not reinforce single women going to the movies or eating out alone. Some people do not approve of single women traveling alone.

Now, as an adult, you are responsible for your own life and you make the rules for your life. No one else can live your life or know what is best for you. So here and now begin to design your life to include traveling alone. Throw away the old restrictions you are hanging on to and begin to experiment with new rules that allow for your personal growth and enrichment.

This section will lead you slowly and comfortably through nine steps of awareness-training and -expanding adventures in familiar surroundings. You will be surprised and delighted by how fast your confidence grows. Your level of discomfort when you go out alone will begin to diminish, and you will soon become competent and confident traveling alone. Like me, you may even begin to *prefer* traveling alone.

STEP ONE

Begin a Travel Notebook

First look around home to see if you have a spiral-bound or sewn notebook that fits into your purse and is large enough to hold more than a few notes. A secretary's dictation book or a small composition notebook works fine, or you may want to buy a "blank book" with an attractive cover. You will now write anything and everything about traveling in this notebook—nothing else.

Carry your travel notebook with you at all times. You never know when an important piece of information will come your way. The travel tidbit may come from someone at work or on TV, or you may read it in a newspaper or magazine. If you do not write the information down in your travel notebook, you may lose it forever.

STEP TWO

Research and Familiarize Yourself with Travel

Schedule one day a week (passionate travelers continue this forever) to go to your public library and read two or more travel sections of large-city newspapers. Give yourself at least two hours to read everything, including the advertisements.

1. Page through the entire section to get a feel for the contents, then return to the first page.
2. Read the feature article. Even though it may be about a place you are not interested in visiting, read for the type of information the writer thinks is important. Look at any sidebars for specific information about hotels, airfares, restaurants and other travel essentials.
3. Read other articles that interest you. Make notes about special events, special fares, and addresses for free information. Continue in this fashion until you have completed reading and making notes on the travel section.
4. Go back to the first page again and read the advertisements. Look for special deals, packages and tours. Sometimes these are the

cheapest way to go, and you don't have to fol-low an itinerary rigorously—you can make your own agenda while taking advantage of the cheaper airfares and hotels.

5. Look specifically at airfare advertisements. Airfares vary widely and are often confusing. A round-the-world ticket may be cheaper than a round-trip fare. Look at the ads and write down telephone numbers for rates that interest you.

6. One more time, return to the first page and survey each page for any information you missed. You may want to make notes concerning travel lectures in your town, local tours, new books, anything that will complete your research for the day.

Remember, make notes about *anything* that inter-ests you: climate, clothing, discount travel agents, travel warnings, new books, free pamphlets…. Don't worry about organizing the material. Date the page in your journal and note the names and dates of the newspapers you reviewed.

Months later, you will remember writing some-thing down, and you will know that you can go to your travel notebook and browse through it for the needed information.

STEP THREE

Begin Awareness Training

At the library, you will begin the first of several awareness exercises. These exercises are designed to increase your ability to use your senses: to see where you are, to know what you are doing *now*, to hear, smell and touch your real world—*to wake up*.

AWARENESS EXERCISE 1: HOW AWAKE AM I?

While sitting in the library, close your eyes and feel the hard/soft seat beneath you.

• Listen to the sounds around you.

• Do you smell anything?

Sit quietly a short while, then open your eyes and begin to look around at the people.

• How many are watching you?

• What are the others doing?

Pick one person and look at him or her very carefully. Let your eyes move slowly from head to feet. Close your eyes again and describe silently to yourself what that person was wearing.

• *Head:* hat, glasses, jewelry?

- *Upper body:* blouse, jacket, long sleeves, dress, overalls? Colors? Textures?

- *Lower body:* pants, skirt, shorts, tights? Colors? Textures?

- *Legs and feet:* hose, short socks, knee-length socks, boots, shoes, sandals, bare feet?

- *Arms and hands:* covered, jewelry, wristwatch?

- Anything else you remember about the person—age, sex, size, pleasant, sad, etc.

Take a deep breath and open your eyes again.

- If the person is still there, what did you miss? And—how well did you remember? How well did you really see that person?

- Were you judging her/him? Is judging a habit?

- Are you judging yourself now? Do you frequently judge yourself harshly?

Close your eyes again.

- Listen to the sounds. Are there new ones? Are some missing? Are the sounds coming from inside the building or outside?

- Do you smell anything? Do you know what it is?

- What is the temperature of the air touching your face? Are your hands or feet cold? Warm?

- Is your posture comfortable? Are you more or less comfortable than you were when you began the exercise?

Open your eyes.

Repeat this exercise often, in other places, really looking at a variety of people. You will be surprised how quickly your awareness becomes sharper—you will see more, hear more, smell more and be much more aware of what your body is touching.

You will begin to wake up—
To your life here, to your life now.

Begin now to travel by experiencing your everyday world with the same awareness with which you hope to experience new and exotic places. Our culture and lifestyle have taught us to turn off our senses and to judge whatever we do sense as good or bad. As a young child all your senses were alive, and you were interested in your world, as it was, without judging. Just as you practice any new or lost skill, you will need to practice sensing with awareness and without judging.

To travel without awareness is a waste of time and money.

STEP FOUR
Go to a Movie

"You wouldn't worry much about what other people think of you—if you only knew how seldom they do."

—Anonymous

Choose a movie and a screening time you prefer: morning, afternoon or evening. Will you go to a nearby movie house or one that's across town? Make the experience as easy on yourself as possible. *Then go.*

Your movie excursion offers a good opportunity to practice your second awareness exercise.

AWARENESS EXERCISE 2: WHO IS WATCHING ME?

Choose a time when you feel uncomfortable or conspicuous. Perhaps you're walking down the street toward the movie theater or standing in line for tickets.

Look around and see what other people are doing. Take your time. When you have finished viewing the scene, ask yourself:

• How many people were watching me?

- How important do I think I am in their lives, now?

- Have my feelings changed? Do I feel more conspicuous? Less conspicuous?

Now close your eyes and sense the *place*—weather, noises, odors, safe, dangerous, pleasant, unpleasant. Keep your eyes closed.

- Is your body tight or relaxed?

- Are your shoulders hunched or relaxed?

- Are your jaws and mouth clenched, open, relaxed, tense?

You don't have to change anything, but you can if you want to. I just want you to begin to be aware of your body—what your body is saying to you, now, in this place, at this time, about this place.

Begin to trust messages from your body.

How was your first solo movie-going experience? What did you feel good about? Give yourself full credit for risking a new and exciting—perhaps even scary—adventure.

What do you want to do differently next time? Go to a theater farther away, across town? Choose a different time? Buy popcorn? Okay. Do it.

It's time now to expand your horizons. Most newspapers have weekly entertainment calendars. Go through your local paper and choose two or three events per week. Include concerts, lectures, poetry readings and art gallery shows. Go by yourself. With such adventures you are already "traveling alone."

Repeat Awareness Exercises 1 ("How Awake Am I?") and 2 ("Who Is Watching Me?").

Continue going to movies, concerts, lectures and other activities in your town, on your own. Anytime you fall back into self-consciousness or other feelings of discomfort, repeat your awareness exercises. At this point you will be able to do them quite rapidly, with amazing results.

STEP FIVE

Go to a Restaurant

This may be the most difficult step for you to take. Again, I urge you to take your time. Go at your own pace. *Respect yourself.* Too often we are tempted to test ourselves beyond our readiness, and we fail, never to try again. Be gentle with yourself—but *do it.*

Choose a restaurant you have never eaten in and the time that feels easiest and safest: breakfast, lunch or dinner. *Then do it.*

Enjoy the experience as much as you are able. If you are more comfortable than you expected, repeat

Awareness Exercises 1 and 2 and see what effect increased awareness has on your pleasure.

Now it's time for a second meal out. Select another restaurant, a different time of day and a different meal. Be sure to carry along a copy of Awareness Exercises 1 and 2.

After you have ordered your meal, take a long, slow look around the room, then begin Awareness Exercise 1. I think you'll be surprised at how much your awareness has improved already. Remember the first time you did this exercise at the library? If time permits, do Awareness Exercise 2.

If you're still waiting for your meal, begin to make up stories in your head about a person in the restaurant who interests you, either positively or negatively. Or think about how you'd redesign the decor of the restaurant. How would you change it? What things would you keep? There are many games you can invent that keep you *present* and *aware* of the life you are living at this moment.

Wasn't this meal more fun? Less stressful? Perhaps even "nothing special"? See how far you've come already?

STEP SIX

Go to an Elegant Restaurant

"Without risk, life is nothing—a dream empty of dreams."

—Eleanora Duse

Pick the fanciest restaurant you can afford, but one in which you have never eaten alone. Choose the day and time you want to eat, preferably evening.

One to three days before the date you selected, call the restaurant and ask for a reservation for one at the time you wish to eat. If you know the restaurant and have a favorite table, ask for it. Make the reservation in your name, first or last or both.

On the day of your reservation, take plenty of time getting ready. Have your hair done, nails, massage—anything that makes you feel beautiful. Maybe even treat yourself to a new dress.

Dress conservatively and elegantly, as you would when traveling out of town or in another country. It's important that *you* be pleased with how you look. You're dressing for no one else. You are your own best friend, and tonight your dinner date is with *you*.

Arrive on time but not early, or you may have to wait. Tell the host, "I have a reservation for 7:30 under the name _____." He or she will lead you to your table or tell you that it's not ready. If your table isn't ready, ask how long it will be before it is. Restaurants can't control when previous diners will leave, but staff can make a good guess. You're asking the question to show the host that you expected your table to be ready at the time of your reservation. Be gracious and reasonable; don't get angry and spoil your evening or make yourself uncomfortable. The host may suggest that you wait in the bar. If you want to, go ahead, but remember that alcohol dulls the senses, and we want this evening to be a sensual experience.

After you've been seated, take your time ordering. Don't be rushed by the presence of the waiter. Ask any questions you have, about the menu, the specials, how a dish is prepared, the size of portions, etc. Ask what is included in the entree price.

Ask anything that will help you make decisions about what you wish to order. *Take your time.*

After you've ordered your meal, try Awareness Exercise 3.

Awareness Exercise 3:
Where Am I?

Relax, lean back in your chair and then look around.

First look at your table:

- *Table:* What is it covered with? Note the color, feel the texture—pleasing? Cheap? Luxurious? Clean?

- *Napkin:* How is it folded? Size? Color? Texture?

- *Silverware:* What kind? How many pieces? Silver? Stainless? Pick up the knife: How does the weight feel? Special handles?

- *Flowers:* Artificial? Fragrance? Vase? Color? Shape? Pick up the vase and smell the flowers.

- What else is on the table? Any new ideas for your home?

Now look around the room. How do the room and decor affect you?

- Check out your body: Relaxed? Soothed? Caressed? Jangled? Cold? Hot? Uplifted? Crowded?

- Are there odors? Noises? Music? Quiet? Activity? Colors?

- Drop your shoulders, take a deep breath and look around *slowly.*

- Who else is here? Slowly count the people in the room. Couples? Groups? Single diners?

- How many people are watching you?

- What colors attract or repel you?

- Whom are you curious about?

- Make up stories about the diners and waitresses.

Some people suggest that you read a book when you eat out alone—I don't agree. If the book is worth reading, it will take you away from your present experience, away from the restaurant and the food you are paying for, paying with time from your life and money from your savings.

Don't cheat yourself.

Be here now.

If you are still waiting for your food, you may want to repeat Awareness Exercise 3 so that your memory of this special night will be full of bright, clear pictures. You'll discover how easy it is for you now to see a richness of details you might have missed a few months ago.

Another way to enjoy and fully remember this important evening is to take a journal with you and write down what you are seeing, feeling, smelling, hearing and touching, as well as any stray thoughts or memories that are triggered by these sensations. Don't let your memories carry you away, though. Be sure to stay here, stay present. Count the people, chairs, blondes—anything to help you stay focused on this present moment in your life.

When your meal arrives, it's time to enjoy. Smile when the waiter proudly sets your food before you, and remember to give thanks to your waiter—and to yourself for taking this risk and treating yourself to this uncommon night out.

Feast your eyes. Be sure to put on your glasses if you need them to see clearly. Take in the colors, textures and the arrangement on the plate, and the design of the plate itself.

Take time.

Can you see a wisp of steam? Smell the tantalizing fragrances? If you can't smell the food, move your face closer to the plate, or lift the plate closer to your face. Is it hot? Cold? Does the food smell as good as it looks?

Take time.

Now you are ready to taste the flavors, feel the textures, listen to the crunch as you slowly savor your food.

Take your time.

Taste each part of the meal separately, then all together if you want. Look at the bread—smell it, feel it, and spread it slowly with the butter.

We need food to survive, physically and spiritually. Eating is a sacred ritual. Everything we eat was once a living plant or animal. Honor their sacrifice with time, appreciation and joy. Eating is entertainment, fun. Make it a sensual delight. (Before your next meal out, rent the movie *Tom Jones* and watch the famous eating scene.) Practice awareness at every meal.

Sometime during your meal, look around and see who's watching you. I hope by now you've learned that most people don't even know you exist and therefore aren't thinking about you at all. I learned a long time ago that no matter what I do, about a third of the people around me approve, a third disapprove and a third don't even know I exist.

When finished with your meal, which may include an elegant dessert with coffee, ask for the check. Your waiter may have already placed it on your table. Do not leave your table until you are absolutely ready, no matter how many people are waiting.

Never skimp on the tip. Don't ruin your luxurious feelings by getting uptight about money now. If it isn't easy for you to figure a fifteen percent tip, carry a pocket-size tip chart.

Congratulations! This meal has been part of your education and an important step toward traveling alone and loving it. You have taken a risk and now have more confidence in yourself. Some of this new experience may have been fun, some of it scary, some of it even boring at times, but *you did it!*

You are now ready for more dining out alone—and for Awareness Exercise 4.

AWARENESS EXERCISE 4: JUST SAY "NO"

This exercise will give you practice in saying "no" to your waiter. Your first "no" may not represent your true feelings; this is just practice. You may do one or all of these suggestions, but practice at least one. The more you practice, the better you will be able to say "no" when it really counts.

- When your waiter shows you to a table, say, "No, I'd rather have that table." No matter what the waiter says, do not accept the first table offered. Even if you have to walk out and go to another restaurant, you will probably discover that nothing spectacular happens. Do not get angry. Just be clear and firm.

- Ask your waiter what he or she recommends: "What do you think is good today?" Then clearly and quietly say, "No, thanks. I'd rather have _____."

Keep eating out and keep practicing. Try a new "no" each time.

- Also practice asking for what you want. For example, ask to have the music turned down or up, the heat or air conditioning turned up or down, or ask to move away from a draft or noise from the kitchen.

Remember, you're paying for your meal with the same currency other people use. Respect your rights and desires. No one else is responsible for taking care of you.

The skill of saying "no" regarding what you don't want, as well as the skill of stating what you *do* want, will be important as you travel—for example, when asking to see a hotel room before you agree to rent one, then asking to see another if the first room doesn't please you. You'll also need to be able to say "no" firmly in popular tourist places with insistent salespersons or beggars: learn to say "no" in the local language, refuse to make eye contact and simply erase them from your consciousness. Don't expect these experienced entrepreneurs to play by your rules, but you don't have to play by their rules either. While you may think them rude, they know from experience that insistent behavior pays off in more business.

STEP SEVEN
Take a Day Trip

See how far you've come! You're beginning to form good travel habits that will serve you well throughout your entire travel life—and you're ready to plan a day trip as if you were going to Europe, even though you'll stay closer to home for now.

Your first trip should stretch you but not overwhelm you, expand your life yet not defeat your motivation.

Here are a couple of warnings about travel "greediness" and waiting. Our irritation while waiting is usually about wanting to do, see or be somewhere other than where we are. We think we won't get enough. I hate waiting. Here are some suggestions for turning waiting into pleasure.

Of course, I always have something to read available. One time I wrote poems while stopped by construction on the highway. The writing helped me see details I would have overlooked. As poetry they won no prizes, but for me they are photographs of both the world around me and the world within me, at that moment. This is a good time to listen to taped stories or language lessons—or even begin your long-awaited novel. I may do short de-stressing procedures: close my eyes and breathe deeply, or say a quieting mantra.

Careful planning before you go will help control your travel greediness. If you're too greedy and try to "see it all," your body will rebel. You may get sick or have an accident because you're tired. Anyway, it would take more than one lifetime to see everything interesting on this magnificent planet.

You won't need to go through each step in the following planning process for your day trip, but I want you to begin thinking ahead and see how your day trip resembles longer and wider travels.

Travel Planning Process—For Any Trip

1. Ongoing research and awareness practice.
2. Choose a destination and set a budget.
3. More research on the selected destination.
4. Choose specifically what you want to see and do, in the order of importance to you. Make a time plan for each day.
5. Transportation: decide how you will get there and how to get around once you are there, to and from the airport, freeway, bus or train station. If possible, obtain maps of streets, bus and subway routes.
6. Where will you sleep? You may want to make a reservation for the first night.

7. Where will you eat? The first meal, and any special restaurant or food you want to try on your trip.
8. Make reservations for transportation, hotels, tours, concerts.
9. Clothes: select appropriate clothes and examine for needed repairs, cleaning, etc.
10. Luggage: during the weeks or days prior to packing, open your luggage in a corner of your bedroom and place in it the travel items you plan to take.
11. Special equipment: depending on your interests and planned activities, acquire hiking stick, binoculars, camera, immersion heater for tea, camping equipment, etc.
12. Review budget: buy traveler's checks, withdraw cash and decide on safe money-carrying plan and container.
13. Pack and repack lighter. Take only what you can easily carry up stairs and lift into an overhead luggage rack.
14. Prepare home for leaving. Make a checklist for your home and for your departure. Stick them both on the door through which you will leave.
15. Before you leave home: Tickets? Money? Reservations?

Make several copies of this outline so you can use one for each trip. Eventually you will develop your own personalized travel plan and checklists.

Make as many decisions as possible before you leave home. Once you arrive at your destination, time is too precious to spend deciding what to do next. You don't have to follow your plan, but it is very important to have one.

When planning a day trip, there are a few important items to think about:

• Decide when you should leave so that you will arrive easily and safely, allowing for unexpected stopovers, meals or rest stops. *Stay aware* as you travel toward your destination; notice people, houses, businesses, parks, trees and flowers. Make the *trip* as important as your destination. Stop along the road and listen to the stream. Get out of the car and smell the pine forest. Take a closer look at roadside flowers. You may even want to take a short detour so that you can walk through a covered bridge.

• What will you eat? Do you want to explore a new restaurant, or buy a gourmet picnic? Plan to eat out for at least one meal. Choose a local, ethnic or unusual cafe. Practice awareness eating.

• When do you want to return? Do you have your bus/train schedules? Avoid commuter rush hours in the morning and evening. An hour earlier or later can make a world of difference.

• What will you wear? The method of transportation you choose and the activity you expect to engage in will determine what you take and wear. Now is the time to begin exploring comfortable, conservative travel clothes. Look in your closet, drawers and shelves and think *layering* for changeable weather and different times of day and evening.

• This is also the time to experiment with suitcases, day packs, fanny packs and backpacks. Ask friends to lend you their favorites so that you can check out what suits you best. Visit travel, sport and luggage stores to see the many items available. Pick them up, try them on, walk about the store.

You'll develop your own basic clothing rules as you travel more. I've developed four:

1. Wear comfortable walking shoes—shoes you've broken in, not new shoes. If you want to buy new walking shoes or hiking boots, ask knowledgeable friends what they wear and perhaps invite them to go shopping with you.

Take an old pair of shoes along on your first day trip, just in case.

2. You should feel attractive, rather than sexy, in what you wear.
3. Mind the weather and be warm enough, or cool enough.
4. Choose your clothes to suit the activities you plan. No tight skirts for horseback riding or easy walking.

What else will you take on your day trip?

• Money is number one. Whatever your budget, be sure to have money in a variety of bills, readily available and safely stored. Keep track of your spending so that you don't come up short. Stash some emergency money.

• Tickets for travel or reserved admission, if needed. If possible, buy your tickets a few days before you plan to leave and put them inside the purse you have decided to take with you.

• Purse, day pack, fanny pack or string sack—something that will hold everything you need for the day. This way, you can easily keep track of camera, sandwich, beverage and travel notebook—all in *one* container.

• Miscellaneous—as few items as possible, depending on your plans. These might include a watch or clock; medicines; cosmetics; a thin, packaged, plastic raincoat; sun hat or warm hat with a brim; gloves; perhaps a camera or binoculars. *Don't overload yourself.*

You may think I'm making much too big a deal out of a simple one-day trip. Well, I am, and it *is* a big deal if you've never made a one-day excursion by yourself. You'll make many such outings during your future travels at home and around the world. Those day trips will have to be just as well organized as this very first one—only by then you'll be able to organize quickly and easily because you began developing good travel habits on your first trip.

Now that you're ready, take three one-day trips and practice the previous awareness exercises.

STEP EIGHT

Make Overnight and Extended Trips; Visit a City

Everything you learned on your day trips is applicable to a weekend or extended trip. You are now rapidly becoming an experienced solo traveler. Just take along more money, decide where you will stay, pack night clothes and a toothbrush, and you're ready to go—or almost. If you plan to visit a city, some special planning will help you make the most of your experience.

Visiting any large city is very much the same, whether it is in the United States or a foreign land. In cities, you'll find many of a culture's or community's outstanding accomplishments—art, historical buildings, cathedrals, sacred places, markets and stores. There's so much to see and do in cities that you'll have to do some pre-trip research and planning.

First, visit the library for more research. Read one or more travel books on the city you are going to—even if it's nearby. Make notes about things you might want to see or do. Photocopy neighborhood maps and enlarge areas you want to visit. Write to state or city tourist information bureaus for the most up-to-date maps. Alternatively, obtain one locally before you depart, or get a map as soon as you arrive at your destination. Car rental companies, hotels and sometimes airport information desks offer free maps. Don't forget the valuable help offered by the American Automobile Association (AAA)—you may want to become a member.

Make a priority list, beginning with the most important and ending with the least important activities you want to experience, sights to see, etc. in the city you plan to visit. Know what you want to do and see *before you leave home.*

Now it's time to schedule your activities:

First day. It is most important to have a plan for your first day, even if it begins at four o'clock in the afternoon. Plan something near your hotel, select a restaurant for supper nearby, or plan to stay in your room to rest or fine-tune your plans for the following days.

Second day, morning. Take a city tour. Try a commercial tour by Gray Lines or another sightseeing company, or call the local bus service to see if they have suggestions for a city tour using public transportation—for example, in New Orleans you might take the St. Charles Avenue Streetcar. A tour will give you a sense of the city, its geography and the places you may want to return to on your own. After the tour you may want to change your overall plan.

Second day, afternoon. Arrange for one or two activities in one part of the city.

Second day, third day, etc. Make a plan for your entire visit. The longer you stay in one city, the more leeway you have in planning your activities. Never let your plan interfere with unexpected opportunities for delight. You may decide to sit at a sidewalk cafe all afternoon watching the life of the city pass by instead of going to an art gallery as planned. Remember, you'll never be able to see or do *everything*.

Last day. This is a crucial day and must be carefully planned. Usually, activities will be dictated by your time of departure.

I pack early, sometimes the night before leaving. Check your ticket to see what time your plane, bus or train departs. Be sure to return your ticket to your valuables pocket (see Part Two: "How to Make Your Own Valuables Camisole").

Some tips on departure:

• Plan to arrive early for your departure. Arrange for transportation to the terminal, if needed.

• If you're driving, plan to give yourself time to depart in an unhurried manner, missing commuter traffic. Leave earlier or later than commuters.

• Before you pay your hotel bill, check to be sure there are no incorrect charges. Don't be bashful—ask for an explanation of any item you don't understand. It's your responsibility and your money. People are basically honest, but they sometimes make mistakes.

• If you want a one- or two-hour delay in vacating your room, ask for it. If you cannot get a delay, then ask the hotel to store your luggage until it's time for you to depart. I've never been turned down when I've asked the front desk to store my luggage until departure, and I've never lost anything that way.

• If there's time, plan some convenient treat. You may want to see or do something, just hang out with a book or write postcards.

• Always travel with a book, or part of a book, for waiting in airport terminals, long tourist lines, etc. Waiting is boring and toxic for me, so I transform waiting time into reading time. Before I leave home, I visit local used bookstores or thrift shops looking for books I didn't get around to reading when they first came out. Or I may find an anthology of short stories or Greek plays—anything that interests me. I tear the book into small segments and staple each segment's pages together. When I go out sightseeing for the day I take only one or two segments—not the whole book. That way I always have something interesting to read without the inconvenience of carrying a heavy book. I do the same with guidebooks, tearing out only what I need for a particular outing.

STEP NINE
Awareness Update

Review and practice your awareness exercises, then stretch your awareness a little further:

• Spend a full day concentrating on your sense of smell. Go to a park and smell the flowers, grass, tree bark, water, rocks, everything. Move about slowly. Next, go to a department store and sample perfume, wander around awhile, then go smell the perfumes for men. Next, go to a restaurant or a grocery store and sample the fragrances there.

• Now take a day for sounds. Concentrate on listening to birds, motors, voices, radio, TV (without looking), wind, leaves rustling, animals, rain, several types of music. Listen, listen, listen.

The following awareness exercise is designed to further your perception of the world you live in and the qualities of your life—here and now.

AWARENESS EXERCISE 5: TOUCH AWARENESS

This exercise can be practiced anywhere. I like to practice in a park or when I am camping. Other good places are department stores, certain museums, your home or your hotel room.

Use your hands first—the part of our body we use to reach out to touch our world. Don't forget to practice with your bare feet, your face and your back. Indeed, learn to become aware of your whole body and how it touches the world.

Touching # 1

1. As you read these words, become aware of the experience of touching. Close your eyes. Begin with your toes—is anything touching them? Shoes? Grass? Carpet?

2. Move slowly up the soles of your feet, ankles, legs, knees, thighs—stopping to sense any awareness of being touched—by air, soft cloth, tight hose, rough fabric, hard seams, heat, moisture, cold.

3. As you sit, how do you experience the touch of the chair or couch? Is there pressure? Softness? Hardness? How about the sides of your buttocks and lower back—can you feel the touch of anything?

4. Is your abdomen billowing out in front of you? Or is it flat and hard? What does it feel like? Relaxed? Tight? Caressed? Restricted? Are your clothes comfortable and nonrestrictive?

5. Place a hand on your chest. Experience its rising and falling as you breathe. How does the touch and weight of your hand feel to the chest? How does the

touch of the chest feel to your hand? Now, take your hand away and become aware of your chest. Are there any constrictions? Soft clothes? Tight clothes?

6. Next, sense your shoulders, arms and hands—in that order. Slowly, with eyes still closed, lift the shoulders as high as possible, up under your ears. Drop the shoulders. What does that feel like? Repeat the lifting and dropping of the shoulders to experience the difference between relaxed and tight muscles. What is touching your shoulders? Upper arms? Forearms? Hands and fingers? Do you feel jewelry? Sleeves? Air? Warmth?

7. With eyes closed, sense your face. What is your expression? Pleasant? Frowning? Corners of the mouth—up or down? Are your lips touching? Teeth touching or apart? Jaws clenched? Can you sense anything touching the skin of your face? Hair? Breeze? Moisture? Dryness?

8. Open your eyes and sit quietly, savoring the awareness of touch.

Touching # 2

Go to your closet, open the door and stand in front of your clothes so that they are within easy reach. Close your eyes. Beginning at the far left, using both hands, hanger by hanger touch the clothes you find there— the fabric, the trim, the sleeves. Pay close attention to the texture of each item. Is it fuzzy? Slick? Soft? Harsh? Rough? Nubbly? Metallic?

Before opening your eyes, stand quietly and become aware of your reaction to this experience.

Open your eyes.

Touching # 3

In your back yard or a park, walk around and touch as many items as you can. Do this for five minutes, touching rocks, tree bark, grass, sand, metal, finished wood, plastic, etc.

Next, pick an object that attracts you—a tree, a rock, a flower, any one item. For a full five minutes (a very long time) touch the object in every way possible. For example—with each finger, back of your hand, face, your back, feet, both hands at once. You will discover many more ways of touching.

Touching # 4

There are many taboos about touching in our culture, and one of the strongest is the taboo against touching oneself. In this exercise I want you to begin to know yourself, your travel companion, through the sense of touch. Sit or stand, in front of a full-length mirror if possible. (Without a mirror is okay.) Touch your hair with both hands—palms, fingers, front, back. Move to your forehead, eyebrows, cheeks, lips, chin, ears, neck.

Retouch any part that interests you or feels especially good.

Continue to explore your body. Take your time. Don't leave any part out. Don't judge. Just experience. Without this body you won't be able to travel, so appreciate it, love it and take care of its needs.

As you go about your regular day's activities, practice your awareness exercises. Begin to see, hear, smell and touch your world.

Awareness of where you are and what you are doing will enrich your life and your travels. The time, money and energy you expend traveling will be worth it.

PART TWO

Tips for the
Solo Traveler

You are no longer a beginner. Spread your wings and travel as far as you want to go. Don't forget to do your weekly library research and practice all of your awareness exercises often. Awareness can never become automatic. When you are on automatic, you are not aware.

Even though this book focuses on traveling alone, most of the ideas are equally valuable when traveling with a companion.

Speaking of companions, anytime on your solo trips you suddenly have a craving for company, it's easy to find. In your hotel, hostel, on local tours, or in restaurants you will see other travelers interested in many of the same things you are. That's why they are there. So speak up. They are often just as shy as you are. Ask them where they live, what they've enjoyed most, what they're seeing or doing today.

If, after talking with fellow travelers, you'd like to spend more time with them (sometimes they're not as interesting as they looked), invite them to meet you for lunch or tell them you'd like to join them on an excursion. If your first invitation doesn't work out, try again. Most people are just as reticent as you are and may really want company too. I've met extremely interesting people this way.

PASSPORT TO ADVENTURE

Do you dream of visiting Europe? South America? Even if your answer is "no" at this time, I suggest that you apply for a passport now. A United States passport is good for ten years.

Something magic happens when you hold that little blue passport in your hand. Suddenly, you are free to travel in and out of the United States at a moment's notice. You are available for any unexpected gift of time or money or ticket. Just rub your hands on the small blue book and it's "Goodbye, Kansas!"

The process of applying for your first passport is easy as well as time-consuming. The cost is $65. First call the postmaster at your local post office to see if he issues passports. If not, he will tell you where to get an application. Important: If you wait for the last minute (i.e., three weeks or less prior to departure), you will be charged *$30 extra* for fast service and may be asked to produce a ticket or itemized travel itinerary. *Don't wait! Get your passport. Do it now.*

You will need:

• Proof of citizenship, usually a birth certificate or naturalization papers.

• Two passport pictures—2 inches by 2 inches—color prints, or black and white. Many film developing studios offer these, as well as the AAA. You can also have someone take your portrait, facing directly into the camera, in front of a plain background—a wall or the side of a building. Smile and wear your hair in a flattering style. This picture will follow you for ten years, so be sure you look your best. When you choose your picture, have six to ten copies made, for visas and to replace your passport if it becomes lost.

• Personal identification such as a driver's license.

• If your present name is different from the one on your birth certificate, things get complicated, so check with the post office or passport office.

• Cash, check or money order for $65.

• A filled-out passport application.

You must appear *in person* the first time you apply for a passport. Future passports can be renewed by mail.

Visas must be obtained from many countries before you visit them, but you do not need a visa at this stage. Wait until you are planning a trip and have specified dates. Often (but not always) visas can be obtained when you arrive in the country you are visiting.

HEALTH AND MEDICAL MATTERS

Some pretrip preparation is needed when it comes to health considerations:

• Be sure, when you're inquiring about visas for travel abroad, to ask what, if any, immunizations may be needed for the countries you plan to visit. Don't leave inoculations to the last minute, in case you suffer any minor discomfort from them.

• When packing for your trip, make certain that you have an adequate supply of any prescription or other medications you normally use, along with any other daily health-care supplies.

• Take along your health-insurance or Medicare card for emergency medical expenses. Does your policy cover you when traveling? If not, consider purchasing traveler's medical insurance, as well as insurance that covers medical evacuation expenses.

• Carry a thermometer on your trip. If you do become ill during your travels, be sure to drink one to four quarts of safe fluids a day and go to bed to rest. If your illness persists, see an English-speaking doctor, but I would advise against receiving any type of injection with needles. In an emergency, call your embassy or consulate.

TRAVEL PLAN

For tips on travel planning, please see "Travel Planning Process—For Any Trip" in "Step Nine: Take a Day Trip" in Part One.

TRAVEL BUDGET

In *Around the World in Eighty Days*, Phineas T. Fogg packs a very large carpetbag full of money—and just takes off. That option is not available to most of us, and the world has changed a bit since the 1800s.

Two ways of money planning are open to you. One method is to count how much money you have, then plan where you can go and what you can do with that amount. The second way is to decide what you want to do and where you want to go, then be sure you have enough money to do it. For most of us, the only way to have money to travel is to save for it. So open a Travel Savings Account at the bank.

I believe we will always have enough money for what we value—it's a matter of priorities. Do we want a new tv...or a trip? A new car...or a cruise? Cigarettes...or health and camping equipment? A fancy apartment...or a trip around the world? There are no "right" or "wrong" choices. But for most of us, choices must be made. Make your choices with awareness.

Budget Planning

Imagine you have $500 to spend on a trip. To get an idea of the kind of trip you are able to make, begin by estimating all the necessary expenses:

Essentials:

Transportation

Plane/train/bus: one-way or round-trip ticket

airport departure tax

airport bus

taxis

local bus/trolley/subway

Automobile

your car—new tires or a tune-up needed?

car rental—check your insurance to see if you're covered when you drive a rental car so you don't have to buy coverage from the rental agency.

gasoline/oil

parking

toll roads

Hotel/motel/camp fee/hostel—per day, times ___ number of days = $____.

Food—cost per day times number of days

Tipping

Optional:

Excursions, local tours

Entertainment, movies, nightclubs, concerts

Special interests, lessons, film

Purchases: Buy useful souvenirs, items such as clothes, towels, purse, luggage, costume jewelry, etc., not tourist trash. If you choose to purchase gifts, apply the same usefulness test. T-shirts are my favorite gifts: they're not very expensive and are easy to carry.

Emergency Funds: Add at least 10 percent to your budget for unexpected expenses. I take more money than I expect to spend, just for the comfort of knowing it is there; then I cash in my leftover traveler's checks when I get home. However, if you're not well-disciplined when it comes to money, then take only what you intend to spend. Carry your credit card or bank card for unexpected needs, and don't forget your medical-insurance card or Medicare card for emergency medical expenses.

The first time you make a travel budget it will be tedious and probably discouraging, but don't let that stop you. With experience you will know what it costs you to travel in the style you are comfortable with.

How I Save Money

My money-stretching habits reflect my preferences. You will develop your own spending plan based on your preferences. My habits include:

• *Sleeping:* Least expensive safe places to sleep: youth hostels, YMCA or YWCA, no-frills hotels and camping.

• *Food:* immersion heater and cup for tea or coffee in my room. I find a grocery store soon after arrival for milk, cereal, fruit for picnic or breakfast/supper in my room. When eating out, I have a large lunch or a "fixed price" meal.

• *Transportation:* Special midweek or off-season rates, senior discounts. Always explore special AAA or business rates, etc. I use local public buses or trains, if at all possible, to and from the airport.

• *The personal splurge:* If I really want a special experience, I include it in my budget. I may sleep at the YMCA but have dinner in the fanciest restaurant in town—if that is my dream. My splurge may be a local tour, a concert, or a carriage ride around the park; a hovercraft boat ride, a day-long tour of Southern mansions, or a visit to a rain forest or a volcano top. Even language classes may be included in my budget.

Be sure you have enough money so that you don't waste time worrying. Keep a careful record of your spending every day and stick to your budget.

LUXURY FOR THE PRICE OF A MEAL

Zacapu, Mexico. I taxied to the hotel I had chosen out of my book, but there were no lights showing—so on to the next one on my list. Hotel Imelda was open, lighted and the room newly refurbished. The building looked as if it was being rebuilt. I was hot, sweaty and tired. I checked if the overhead fan worked—it did. So I rented my two-bed room with bath for $16.60. I walked across the street and bought a quart of leche fria, cold sterilized milk, and sweet Mexican pastries (pan dulce) for my supper and rehydration.

After I drank a whole quart of milk with pastries, I took a shower, soaked a towel and wrung it out, and went to bed. I slept well with the wet towel on top of me and the overhead fan running on medium. I didn't know if I would feel like going to the beach the next day or not. I felt as if I had really done a stupid thing, coming so far on a bus for just one day at the beach. Yet no one could have talked me out of it. I had to try.

Next morning I was up at seven and out look-ing for the local bus to Ixtapa. I found one just three blocks away. By eight I had ridden down the whole mile or so of Ixtapa's fancy-expensive hotels and picked a place to get off. I walked straight through the lobby of the Omni hotel, as if I were a hotel guest coming in from an early-morning walk, greeted the doorman and went on out to the beach, where I selected a hotel palapa *(palm shel-ter) as the attendant brought me a chair. I tipped him and settled in for the day. All the beaches in Mexico are public, but I was sitting in the hotel's private area behind a fence.*

After I had arranged my things in the palapa, *I started down the beach for a two-mile walk. (I had, of course, taken my valuables with me.) My body felt amazingly good.*

I was plenty tired when I returned, ready to "set a spell." I went to the hotel's splendid shaded patio cafe and had a huge breakfast of fresh sliced pineapple, huevos *(eggs)* rancheros, *sweet rolls and a tall glass of fresh-squeezed orange juice, fol-lowed by many cups of good coffee. I made break-*

fast last at least two hours, as I watched the ever-changing blue sea caress and pound the sandy beach. Then back to the beach chair—for the remainder of the day. I stayed put until 6:00 P.M.

I accomplished a lot on this doing-nothing day. I spent time reading and writing. I dozed from time to time, or watched the bathers flirt with the high waves or fly through the air in a parachute pulled by a speedboat. A sailboat slipped across the far horizon. A large cruise ship moseyed by. A few jet skis polluted the air with their racket. Children played in the sand. I was one of four gringos I saw all day. It is off-season in Ixtapa until the prices go up December 14. From April 15 to December 14 the fancy hotel rooms are half price.

I chose not to go snorkeling at a nearby island, even though I'd heard the snorkeling was excellent. The waves seemed too high for swimming at this beach this day. Besides, I had the next day's bus trip to look forward to.

I returned to my hotel as the orange sun slipped silently into a darkened sea. I repeated the previous night's supper and sleeping arrangements. I was up and on a bus by 6:30 A.M. for my four-

teen-hour ride back to Zacapu. I was glad to get back "home" to cooler air.

WHAT WILL YOU WEAR?

As a frequent traveler I'm always on the lookout for travel items. That way I never need to go out and buy a new outfit just before taking a trip. I keep my travel clothes and gadgets packed in one place, either a travel drawer in my dresser or stored in a suitcase or box.

My favorite "travel stores" are Goodwill and the Salvation Army. I have purchased dresses, blouses, raincoats, coats, and once—for six dollars—a fine wool suit. At the Goodwill in Sarasota, Florida, I found a gown and robe set, as well as a perfect paisley-print long-sleeved dress I use for sleeping when I am in a shared-bath hostel.

You'll need two basic wardrobes: one for cool-to-cold weather and one for warm-to-hot weather. Many items can be used in any climate with layering.

Do not take anything you have never worn. Wear the item for at least two to five *long days*. Shoes should be worn for a much longer time. Be sure to walk a total of at least fifteen miles in them with soft, clean socks or stockings. I use thin cotton anklets, white or black, and rarely wear nylon knee-length or panty hose except for dressy occasions. (Even then I am more apt to wear flat sandals without hose.) Once a year I home-dye anklets, hose, or whatever I need that I have not been able to find in black. Rinse well. Be sure the colors are not going to run when washed—and be sure to wash everything before you leave on a trip.

What you wear depends, first, on your feeling good and attractive in what you are wearing so that you can wear it several days and not get too bored; second, on the weather; and third, on what you plan to do in it.

Three Guiding Principles for Clothes Selection

1. *Conventional,* decent, inconspicuous attire coordinated by color. I wear black and navy blue for much of my traveling, and beige, white or pastels for hot climates. I take a plastic zip-lock bag full of colorful scarves to stave off monotony.

2. *Comfortable* in fit, and *appropriate* for the climate and activity chosen. Be creative. I have one long polyester dress with a beautiful print that I love. I wear it to bed and to the shower, on the beach over my bathing suit *and* to the fanciest dinner or concert. It never wrinkles and seems to be indestructible. I haven't tired

of it after years of wear. I am frequently complimented by friends and strangers on how nice I look or how pretty the material is.

3. *Sturdy* garments keep their shape and remain nice-looking even when you wear them day after day after day.

My Choices in Travel Clothes

For me, traveling is not a fashion show. I want to feel well-dressed, but save my newest, most flamboyant fashions for my home turf. As you travel you will develop your own ideas of what you like to wear and will discover those things that are important for *you* to take. Here are some ideas that work for me:

• *Underwear:* two or three pairs of underpants in cotton or silk for good ventilation and evaporation. With just two pairs, I wash one pair and wear the other. If it's my day to move on to another hotel, I put the clean, wet pair in a plastic bag and later hang them up to dry, either in the car or as soon as I check into my new room.

• *Warm wear:* I never leave home without one or two pairs of lightweight long johns and long-sleeved tops in navy blue or brilliant Caribbean color. I wear them alone with a long overblouse, or under my usual clothes. They also make excellent cold-weather pajamas when camping or sleeping in a cold room. I also take a balaclava, or stocking hat, to wear when I camp in a very cold place.

Layering is the way to deal with changes in temperature. If I expect really cold weather when sailing, skiing or trekking high in the mountains, I add clothing made of bunting cloth, even though it is bulky, then cover it all with windbreaker pants and top.

• *Shoes:* This is the hardest adjustment for me to make. I *love* shoes and boots. My closet is full of them. However, I discipline myself and agree to wear one pair of shoes—low-heeled laced walking shoes are a must—to *all* of my city activities. If I weaken and take a second pair, it's flat, lightweight soft-leather sandals or ballet shoes for dress.

If I know I'm going to the beach, I take zorris or beach slippers. If my main activity will be walking in the country, I take a good pair of high-top hiking boots, as lightweight as possible. If I expect to walk in the country only one or two days, I stick with my city walking shoes.

As you can see, shoes are an important item in determining the joy and comfort of your trip. Select them carefully. If you already have good shoes that will serve you well, do not buy new ones. You may want to have the heels renewed, even the soles, and be sure to polish them well. Shoes are not the place for too thrifty budgeting.

• *Dresses, pants, skirts:* Do not change your usual style of dress, but do leave short-short skirts and shorts at home. I do miss my colorful outfits when traveling, but traveling alone I am committed to conservative, unobtrusive, good quality, comfortable clothes. I make most of my own travel clothes, using suitable fabrics I find on sale.

For day wear I do not choose dresses, because I want to be able to easily reach the extra money and valuables I carry in a pocketed camisole under my blouse. With the separation at the waistline between blouse and skirt or pants, I can turn toward a wall or post, reach under my blouse and get my traveler's checks, credit card, passport or whatever I need. If I wear a dress, I must find a restroom or other private place where I can pull my dress up to obtain the needed valuables.

• *Wet–weather wear:* I keep a large, black-plastic garbage bag, with cut-out neck and arm holes, rolled up tight in my purse for an emergency raincoat. There are also thin, light, packaged plastic raincoats that can be used for the same emergencies and take up little room in your purse.

If you expect rain, go prepared with rubber or plastic boots or shoe covers. A raincoat can double as a robe or poncho; a rain hat with a brim can double as a sun hat. A small folding umbrella will fit easily into most purses.

Layer your clothes to stay warm. Cold and wet is a downer even in the loveliest of places.

In tropical countries it rains often, but the rain is warm and pleasant, and your clothes will dry quickly. So don't bother with rain gear, or bring no more than a folding umbrella (for sun *or* rain).

• *Day carryall, travel vest or purse:* My travel vest or day pack will carry *today's* needs only. I take with me: money for today, a travel guide or today's itinerary, currency-converter table, a folding umbrella, glasses, pen and notebook, address book, camera, extra film, ear plugs, aspirin, hard candy, spoon, small Swiss Army knife and a bottle opener. I keep a book, or part of a book, handy if I expect "waiting time." If I'm going shopping, I carry a string bag or day pack.

I learned to use a fishing vest—made of an attractive silver-gray net fabric, with four bulky pockets in the front and one large, flat pocket in the back—as my day "carryall." All of the items listed above fit in the pockets, plus the large back pocket will hold a notebook, extra sweater or wind jacket. The vest thereby takes the place of purse and day pack. I wear the vest inside out so there is more security for my money— and it looks better. My hands are always free, and I don't have to worry about putting my purse or sweater down and walking off and leaving it.

For winter travel I added large pockets to the inside of my jacket to carry all my day's needs. It works just like the vest but is bulkier.

AFFAIRS OF THE HATS

A wide-brimmed, deep-crowned vinyl hat shaded me from the hot sun for the eight-and-a-half years I lived in Bangladesh (then East Pakistan). If a monsoon overtook me, the smooth, soft vinyl hat protected my face from the rain. I had put an elastic chin strap on the hat so it would not sail away in the wind. It was shaped much like a bonnet and was really a high (or medium high) fashion hat in the early days in the manufacture of fine plastics. I could fold it and pack in my suitcase and count on it to pop back into shape.

When I returned to live in the United States my hat was getting a bit scarred and I had little need for such a hat…but I couldn't give her up. By now she was more than a friend; she was family. So I folded her away and kept her under the seat in my Volkswagen camper for years. It was only recently that I buried her, bent and battered, in a garbage can.

The next memorable hat was—no, is—my navy-blue cloth hat with a narrow brim. The only significant characteristic is a small zippered pocket in the headband, for mad money or a car key. I sewed a half-scarf around the base of the hat. With the scarf tied under my chin, the hat is firmly attached against all wind, the back of my neck protected from the biting sun. I have a great picture of me marching briskly along the dock on the way back to my Greek cruise ship in Rhodes.

That hat is now part of my protective, if unattractive, snorkeling costume. When I wear a long-sleeved turtleneck T-shirt and my faithful blue hat, I can snorkel as long as I wish without fear of sunburn.

And then there was the pink straw hat that lay in wait for me. I paused in my last-minute shopping to stare at the brilliant broad-brimmed hat, perched high atop a hat stand filled with somber brown, black and navy-blue felt hats, all ready for the fall and winter crowds. It was September, and any self-respecting summer hat had already gone south for the winter. I, too, was about to leave for Mexico, but I could feel the stirrings of a new love affair.

Magnetically she drew me close and, of course, was a perfect fit. I did not try to escape her charms and docilely asked the clerk the price of this jewel. The clerk didn't know and, like me, could find no tag or markings inside the hat. A second clerk was consulted, with the same results. An hour had gone by as the hat teasingly refused to be priced.

The department manager happened to pass by on her way to lunch. She punched a few codes into the computer and shook her head. "No luck." She handled the hat, scrutinizing it for a clue. Finally, she said, "I think they were on sale for ten dollars. Anyway, you can have it for ten dollars." I said, "sold," and walked out with my new hat—not straw, but a "straw" made of polypropylene. I wondered, "Is this lovely pink creation a reincarnation of my much-loved white vinyl hat of long ago?"

LUGGAGE

Everyone has a different view about luggage. My view is that luggage is a convenient way to carry and protect my things while traveling. It says *nothing* about who you are…how important you are…or how rich you are.

Therefore, if you need to buy luggage, I suggest you start looking for *used* luggage. Goodwill, Salvation Army and garage sales are good places to find excellent luggage, especially hard-sided luggage. (You'll seldom find good soft-sided bags at those places. I don't know why.)

I recommend used luggage because your beautiful new bags will arrive badly scuffed *after your first plane trip*. Also, you need to travel for a while to find out what type of luggage you need for *your* travel style (and how important it is to travel light).

From the very beginning of your travels think *small*. Even when you're traveling by automobile, you'll have to carry your bag or bags in and out of hotel and motel rooms, often up and down stairs. Take only what *you can easily carry* and what *you can lift* into overhead luggage racks.

When you travel by airplane, I advise taking only what you can carry on, if at all possible. Therefore, purchase a soft-sided bag whose dimensions are no larger than a total of forty-five inches when you add length plus width plus thickness. (These are the airline requirements for carry-on luggage; in addition you may carry on a purse and a camera.) Even with this modest luggage load, I use a lightweight luggage carrier with sturdy wheels. A backpack with the above dimensions is also a good carry-on choice. Choose a backpack with an internal frame and, if possible, a side handle for hand carrying—like a suitcase.

One of the delights of traveling is seeing what other people choose for luggage. How do they handle heavy items? Is it really worth the effort to carry on your luggage, as opposed to checking it?

If you do check your luggage, be sure it is labeled inside and outside with your name and address. Lock your bags to discourage theft. However, *never pack or take anything valuable traveling*. Unnecessary valuables rob you of the time and energy required to protect them or even keep track of them.

Mark your bag with bright tape or yarn tassel for easy identification. Baggage-claim areas can be wild and crowded—exciting if you're not in a hurry. You may want to make a simple rip-stop nylon bag to fit over your luggage. Tied with a drawstring through the suitcase handle, the cover will provide additional protection for your suitcase when you check it on a plane or bus.

PROTECTING YOUR VALUABLES

Pouches that hang from the neck, fit inside bras or attach to the legs, as well as money belts of many shapes and materials, exist for your selection. Almost any of them work well if used properly. Shop around; talk to friends. *Whatever you choose must be worn at all times.*

My Way

Under my blouse I wear a pocketed camisole made of cotton or silk for hot climes, or of polyester for cooler places. The first one I made was from an old cotton dress with Philippine embroidery I did not want to throw away. The second was polyester with open-mesh work on the sides for air circulation. The third is a black silk teddy, remodeled. I usually take two on a long journey.

In the front pockets I keep traveler's checks, cash, passport and credit cards. In back pockets I place airplane tickets and extra cash. This is a fairly thick pocketful, which fits easily in the small of my back.

In my travel vest or outside carryall, I keep only the amount of money I expect to spend *that day*. If I need any of the items in my safety camisole, they are easily available under a loose blouse or shirt.

If I remove a credit card or passport, I return it to its safe pocket at once. You may feel awkward doing this in public, but you're not exposed in any way, and only a few people, at most, will notice.

I wear this "valuables camisole" and its contents *at all times*. I even sleep in it. I remove it only to take a shower, and then I keep it within sight in the shower cubicle.

My valuables are always safe from casual theft. If I lost everything else, the contents of my camisole would enable me to continue my trip. Most importantly, I don't have to wonder or remember where my valuables are, thus saving energy—and my attention— for other travel delights.

How to Make Your Own Valuables Camisole

The finished camisole will be long enough to reach about an inch above your waistline. Under a loose blouse, the camisole should not be seen when you raise your arm straight up.

The turned-up section (see instructions, below) will make two or three pockets in front and one in the center of your back, with two pockets on the sides. Close the top of each pocket with Velcro, or with zippers.

The closed pockets should be at least 5 1/2 inches deep, so that passport, traveler's checks, cash, credit cards and airplane tickets will fit inside.

1. Cut the dress, teddy, or material so it hangs from the shoulders to about 5 inches below the waist.

2. Make a 1/2 inch hem at the bottom edge, wrong side out.

3. Turn the hemmed bottom edge up to form a 5 1/2-inch pocket all around the camisole and pin in place. In front, mark two pockets 8 inches wide. In the center of the back, mark a pocket 10 inches wide. This will leave a pocket on each side.

4. Open the edge and sew a lightweight zipper or Velcro on matching surfaces to make secure closures for the pockets.

5. With zipper in place and pocket closed, test to be sure your passport and airplane ticket fit inside the pockets. Stitch the marked sides of the pockets, reinforcing at the top.

6. Try on for fit and relative comfort. Wash before wearing.

Safekeeping Valuables at the Beach

The sea—actually, any body of water—seems to call passionately to most people. Thousands wend their way to the beaches every year. For the solo traveler, the beach presents a special challenge.

It took me years to discover a way to swim at a public beach *and* protect my valuables. A waterproof pouch, sold for cameras, solves the problem. The pouch comes in various sizes and is sold at camera shops. I bought one large enough to hold a small camera and all of my valuables: money, passport, car keys. I place my rolled up "valuables camisole" into a ziplock plastic bag before putting it into the pouch, seal the opening of the pouch as instructed, inflate with air and take it swimming with me.

A handy strap is attached. However, I took a plain white long-sleeved snorkeling T-shirt, made a pocket large enough to hold the inflated pouch, arranged drainage channels and sewed it to the back of the T-shirt. With my valuables pouch safely in the pocket, my hands are free to swim and play. The inflated pouch even makes my body more buoyant.

Now you can buy waterproof pouches with belts, like a fanny pack. They work the same as my T-shirt pocket.

PERSONAL SAFETY

Fear is the major reason most of us put off traveling alone—or even traveling in a group. Fear of the unknown is a normal human emotion we experience each time we try something new: a new job, a new friend, a new style of dress. The unknown is *scary*—and *exciting*. You can go ride a roller coaster and experience fear and excitement, and nothing else. Or go traveling—you will feel fear, excitement and much, much more.

Facing Your Fears

If you are clearly in danger—threatened by a real person, here and now—you probably know what to do, such as yelling "Fire!" or "Help!" or employing the techniques you learned in a women's safety or self-defense class. The response to real danger is no different when you're traveling. The best defense is to stay away from obviously dangerous areas. But no place is totally safe, so don't let your fears stop you from living. Develop a posture that projects confidence, stand tall, know where you are and where you are going. *Expecting to be safe* is an important safety measure.

Most of the time, it is fear of something happening in the future that we fill our lives with. For example, my daughter and I were in a small boat tossed about by a rough Sea of Cortez. I had confidence in the boat handler, but discovered that my daughter was extremely frightened. I told her to look at the shore nearby and count the trees. She began to feel better, and sure enough we landed safely.

Here is a method of dealing with *fear of the future* and any other obsessive or disturbing thoughts.

• Look around and start saying *out loud* what you see: "I see a yellow line in the road with empty spaces in the paint. A red pickup is in front of me. The license plate is RW79-352. Tall fir trees are in the distance..." It sounds weird, but it truly works. This method is also an excellent way to leave work at the office. Practice on your way home. Try it today. See what happens.

• If you're in a crowded elevator or other place where you do not want to speak out loud, then say the words to yourself: "This man's cuffs are frayed and dingy. His pants are blue, and he is wearing brown shoes. I see a pair of red high-heeled shoes, a pair of running shoes. The light is showing floor number 7…" It may sound strange, but try it the next time you find yourself becoming anxious.

My Safety Rules

We live in one of the most dangerous countries in the world. Even so, I live my life freely and with very little fear. That does not mean that I live foolishly, without taking responsibility for my own safety. When I travel I live by a set of rules that have become second nature to me:

• I dress conservatively and inconspicuously.

• I *never* wear expensive jewelry. Leave it *all* at home.

• I keep passport, money, credit card, traveler's checks and plane ticket *on my body at all times*. Even in bed at night or when I go to the shower, I keep them in sight.

- I rarely go out after dark. My days are so well filled that I enjoy quiet evenings in my room, going to sleep early so as to get an early start on the next day's schedule. If I feel I must go out to a special concert or other happening, I try to find another traveler to go with me, *and* I take a taxi to and from the happening.

- I park for rest, camp and sleep *only* where other people are nearby, often at roadside Rest stops, never on a lonely road shoulder. Another place I feel safe is under a bright light in the parking lot of a hospital or grocery. One of the advantages of staying in youth hostels is that you share a room with other travelers, and the building is securely locked.

- I politely ignore all male advances, and, if necessary, say clearly and firmly, "No, thank you. I *never* mix traveling with romance."

- If I find myself in a neighborhood where I become fearful, I imagine lighted candles on both my shoulders, then stand tall and walk rapidly and purposefully toward my destination. I also picture myself, in detail, arriving safely. (Practice seeing such pictures in your mind's eye. See yourself driving into your own garage, or arriving at your destination.)

- To the best of my knowledge, I obey all the rules of dress and behavior of the country in which I am visiting. Usually people are accepting of a tourist's behavior, but I try not to strain that acceptance. I never wear shorts on the street, or in stores or restaurants, or in hotel lobbies, except at beachside resort hotels.

• I choose not to go to a country presently experiencing an internal or external war.

You must make your own rules for safety. Do not be overwhelmed by sensational newspaper headlines. On the day *one* American is killed by terrorism in a foreign land, many are murdered in the United States, and most frequently by family and friends. Your death in an airplane crash is far less likely than being killed driving on U.S. highways.

Although I do follow my own rules, I have no fear of dying while traveling. I know that I will not get out of this life alive, and what a way to go—having a good time.

Living is dangerous. Not to live is death. Live sensibly and with care, at home and abroad.

Whatever your good sense tells you to do in the United States to protect yourself, that same good sense will serve you well in foreign countries. So be sure to take your good sense with you when you go traveling.

HOW WILL YOU GET THERE?

Your library research, travel desires, and, if you so choose, the advice of a travel agent will help you decide the best way to reach your destination. Once you've arrived, you also have choices about how to get around.

Public Transportation

Local public transportation is often the best way to get a close-up look at new places you're visiting in your home state or country, or abroad. It's usually the least expensive way to travel and (but not always) the most efficient. Research your options as much as possible before leaving home.

How to Rent a Car

Public transportation is the cheapest way to move about, but sometimes "you can't get there from here"; so renting a car is the next best choice. Renting your first car can be confusing and even a little scary. Here are some guidelines:

• Don't pay the full rental rate if you can help it. Use your membership in the AAA or AARP, "mileage plus" awards, senior discount or your company card to get a business rate (even though you're not traveling on business).

• Shop around. Look in the travel section of the Sunday newspaper for specials, then call several companies for their prices. Prices vary for different size cars. Also, there are:

Daily rates: the highest rate.

Weekend rates: usually a very good rate, and some companies begin their weekend rates on Thursday. Ask and be clear when the "weekend" rate begins and ends.

Weekly rates: if you plan to keep the car for five days or more, the weekly rate will be the least expensive.

Monthly rates: be sure to check these out if you're going on a long trip.

• Call your own car insurance company to see whether your car insurance covers a rental car with you as driver. Also check your credit card companies to see if they provide car insurance when you charge your rental car on their card. Most people are covered one way or another, and this coverage could save you a lot of money.

• I choose the smallest, cheapest car. Such cars are often in short supply, so be sure to make a reservation as soon as your travel plans are completed. You may be given a larger car for the same price when you pick up your car. By all means, take it—but be sure they charge you the smaller-car rate

• Take your time when you pick up your rental car. Check your time of departure. Since rental companies charge strictly by the 24-hour day, it may be better to eat lunch and spend a little time in the airport now and be able to return the car at a time convenient to your departure time.

• Take the time to *understand your rental contract.* For example, as I already mentioned, if you're covered by your own insurance, make sure you're not paying for the rental company's insurance.

• Before you drive away from the rental company lot, check:

1. The keys in the ignition, and in the trunk, and in the doors. Lock and unlock all three. Is the gas tank full?
2. How to start the motor and how to remove the key from the ignition.
3. Test operation of turn signals, horn, trunk release, fuel door, gas-tank cap, lights, windshield wipers, radio.
4. Does the air conditioner and/or heater work?
5. Adjust the driver's seat, rear-view mirror and side mirrors.

6. Examine the tires. Be sure the car has a spare tire and a jack. You may be surprised to see your first tiny spare tire. Yes, they do work—but don't drive too fast on them.

7. Walk around the car and examine the body. Be sure that any scratches and dents are noted on your rental agreement. Otherwise the rental company can charge you for dents and scratches you did not cause.

• If something goes wrong with the car—if it overheats, or the brakes stop working, or the steering shakes—call the rental company and insist that a replacement car be delivered to you.

• Be sure to return your car on time. If your contract says 9:50 A.M., don't arrive at 10:00 A.M. or you may be charged for an additional day.

• Fill the gas tank *before* you return the car; it will be cheaper than if they fill the tank upon your return.

DIFFICULT DAYS

Your "worst fears" are most unlikely to occur during your travels if you stay aware and follow the advice in this book. Begin to practice the awareness exercises, exercise regularly and eat a low-fat, low-sugar diet *before* you travel. Eat well and continue your exercises while you're traveling, and be sure to get sufficient rest. Don't be greedy and wear yourself out. And remember that there are two difficult days in every trip that demand special alertness and awareness.

Your day of arrival and your day of departure are your most difficult travel days. These are the most tiring and expensive days, and the days you are most apt to lose important items. To reduce the number of such stressful days, I urge you to stay at least four days in each place you stop. When departure and arrival occur in the same twenty-four hours, the problems and stress of that day are doubled.

Take your time. Give yourself time to move slowly. Plan ahead.

Arrival Day

Take your time. Go slow.

A new place is *always* confusing. You *are* disoriented, even when you return to a city or airport you have visited before.

There is a hustling, hurried, high-energy atmosphere all around you. Take a deep breath, try to enjoy waiting for your luggage and locate the transportation desk. Don't get talked into a taxi if you already have an airport bus plan. If it's 3:00 A.M. you may want to hang out at the airport for a few hours, have breakfast, review your plans and save the cost of a hotel room. Or you may be so tired you're glad to go straight to the hotel for whatever rest you can get. Either way is *okay*. This is *your* trip.

Arrival in a Foreign Country

Arriving in any new country is basically the same. Even so, I am always struck by the amount of excitement and fear surrounding the anticipated arrival.

• Be sure to have filled out any arrival forms the airline has given you. I fill them out as soon as I get them to be sure I have all the information I need. Immigration will want to know your name, passport number, where the passport was obtained, when it was issued or when it expires, where you were born and when, what country you are a citizen of and where you live, the number of your flight and the place from which you disembarked. In addition, there may be a customs form—anything to declare? (You will seldom have anything to declare, except when you come back to the United States.)

• When you're on the ground, have your passport in your hand and read the signs, then choose the shortest line for foreigners. There may be a separate line for persons who already have a visa. Nowadays most countries will issue a visa, stamped onto a page in your passport, when you arrive. There is almost always a fee of some kind. (The most I have paid was $20 in Cambodia.) You may be asked how long you plan to stay.

• Next comes customs, where you must collect any luggage you have checked and take it to one of the counters. You may be waved through with a pleasant greeting. Your bags may be searched. In either case, you are now officially a visitor in a new country.

• If you've made arrangements to be met, look for someone holding up a sign with your name on it. It is a most welcome and reassuring sign.

• If you're not being met, your next task is to get transportation to where you want to go. You *must* have a plan of how and where you want to go long before you arrive. Sometimes your plans don't materialize, so you need an alternative plan. I do extensive preplanning using *Lonely Planet* and *Let's Go* guides. Written in my little notebook—before I leave home—is a list of three places I might stay, with their addresses and telephone numbers. Recently, in Singapore, my first selection was the YWCA. When the taxi arrived at the address, it was a bare construction site. My next selection was the YMCA. There were no dorm rooms available, and the price of a private room was $75! So on to my third choice, the Majestic Hotel in Chinatown. I spent a good air-conditioned night in this clean, seedy-looking place—for $47.

• If you're energetic, you may be willing and able to take cheap public transportation when you arrive. Whatever you save in money, you spend in energy and time. Only you know which is best for you. When I arrive I usually take a taxi from the airport to my hotel.

Departure Day

As I said earlier, try to plan your trip so that you have as few of these days as possible. The fewer places you visit, the more you will remember. It's hard for your mind to keep things straight during stimulus overload from the "It's Tuesday, this must be Belgium" syndrome.

Checklists are helpful.

Leaving Your Hotel Room Checklist

• Bathroom and shower for personal articles, behind the door for anything hanging on a hook, and in the shower for shampoo. I never put anything into the medicine cabinet, but try to keep everything out in plain sight.

• Every drawer and closet, even though you don't think you used them.

• Under the bed, on both sides.

• Top of the bed, straighten covers and shake the top one.

Valuables Checklist

• Ticket: Be sure to put it back into a safe place.

• Money: Count all your money, including traveler's checks. How much do you have? Enough for airport departure tax? Local currency? U.S. currency? Traveler's Checks? This is a good time to be sure you have crossed off the traveler's check numbers you've used and compare how much you've spent with your budget.

• Taxi or other transportation money handy?

• Hotel bill paid? Hotel key returned?

• Passport: make sure you have it.

Luggage Checklist

• Number of pieces? Include your purse, camera and any other item you're carrying, so you have *one total number* to remember.

• Combine items to make the number as small as possible. The fewer pieces you have to keep track of, the less stress you'll experience. Also, you're less likely to lose anything from forgetfulness or theft.

• Is your luggage locked? Do not put anything of value or any of your travel documents in luggage to be checked. Locks discourage casual theft but do not protect you from a serious thief.

Be sure to give yourself *plenty* of time to get to the airport or bus or train, well in advance of departure time. If you're leaving by plane, new security regulations may require additional time for checking in. I prefer to be very early so I can avoid the crowd and move smoothly through the check-in process, then have quiet time for meditation, reading, eating or just watching people.

TRUST THE LOCAL PEOPLE: ASK FOR HELP WHEN YOU NEED IT

My grandson and I arrived at Rome's central railroad station just after dark—the wrong time to arrive. Pulling our luggage on wheels along the narrow broken sidewalk, we set out to find our nearby pension. We kept walking and turning, it got darker and darker, and soon I had lost all sense of direction. We could not find our street.

In desperation I turned to a man and woman standing on the corner in the light shining through the door of a small store. With no Italian, I tried to explain our situation by showing them the address of my pension. In my best pantomime I made circles around my head with flying hands, hoping I was letting them know I was confused and lost—not crazy. Our luggage, manner and tired looks all identified us as tourists.

The couple did not seem to know where the address was, but took my piece of paper into the store and consulted the clerk, who began to point and wave her hands. The man emerged from the store and motioned for me to follow him. He stayed several steps ahead of us and walked at a very rapid rate. I suspect he was as uneasy about us as we were about him.

After running to keep up and struggling to keep our luggage from toppling onto the rough sidewalk for many blocks and almost as many twists and turns, we arrived in front of a very tall building. It was old and had a dusty look, with a busy video-game parlor going full blast next door. Truly, two worlds—the old and the new Rome living together. When our guide had confirmed the address, he motioned for us to follow him inside.

There, without hesitation or explanation he squeezed the two of us, along with our bags, into a narrow iron cage, closed the door, dropped a coin in the slot, pushed a button and sent us up in a strange elevator to an unknown floor and an unknown future.

It was the right place and the owner was expecting us. I had sent money and a request for a reservation before we left the United States. All was in order, except...I had been too bewildered to thank the kind gentleman from Rome.

WHERE WILL YOU STAY?

If your plan includes staying overnight, or over many nights, the question of where to sleep must be answered. Are you camping? Do you want to stay in a posh resort? A hotel or motel? A youth hostel? A pension? The "Y"? A bed and breakfast?

The answer will depend on your budget, the available facilities and what you want to see and do. Are you visiting a large city and want to be downtown? If so, a hotel, the YMCA, or a youth hostel may be your choice. Once I stayed in an inexpensive "bed sitter" (room with a hot plate) in the suburbs of London near an Underground station; I could quickly reach the center of town on the Underground.

I have found the *Lonely Planet* and *Let's Go* guides very dependable when it comes to budget hotels. For accommodations that are a step up in price, Frommer's guides are excellent, especially the "Readers recommend" section. Your travel agent will be very helpful in finding the most convenient place to stay in the commissionable category of hotels, with no extra expense to you.

Hotel

If you want to stay in a hotel, visit one or more travel agents until you find one who works well with you. The travel agent will only make reservations with hotels that pay a commission, not YMCAs and youth hostels or many cheaper hotels. However, if you cultivate a relationship with a good travel agent, he or she can help a lot, and there is no charge to you. Your travel agent may be able to find a special package that includes air travel and a hotel within your budget.

• Tell your agent exactly what you want to spend, where you want to go and what you want to do there.

• Always ask about special rates: weekend, senior, student, AAA, business, etc.

• Most of the chain hotels, such as Motel 6 in the United States, provide free catalogs of their franchises so that you can make your own reservations. Stop at a near-by budget chain hotel/motel and ask for the catalog, or ask the desk clerk to make your reservation for you.

Bed and Breakfast ("B&B")

In the United States these popular places range from homes to historical buildings, luxurious mansions and restored country inns. The rates vary as much as the ambiance. Though the prices tend to be on the high side, remember you will probably have a sumptuous breakfast, often eliminating the need for lunch. Foreign countries offer similar accommodations, called pensions.

Check with your travel agent to see if he or she can book you into a B&B of your choice, or check out the B&B books for the region you'll be visiting and book a reservation directly. There is often a B&B reservation service available.

Arrive as early as possible to get the most pleasure out of your stay. Like a resort hotel, a B&B offers a unique experience you do not want to rush. Make the B&B a highlight of your travel, not just a place to sleep.

NOT WHAT I EXPECTED

Old-fashioned windmills stood like ghostly guardians as my plane circled for a landing. I had arrived on the Spanish island of Majorca, home of Majorca pearls.

Customs and immigration went easy and with address in hand, I approached a waiting taxi driver and asked "Cuánto?" We agreed on a price and I climbed into the taxi. He pulled up in front of a very small house, not far from the center of Palma. It was supposed to be the home of an artist who rented one room to tourists at a very reasonable price.

I had phoned ahead from the airport, so Mr. Gabriel was expecting me. With a gracious, friendly manner he showed me to my "room." My surprise must have shown on my face as he hastily picked up my bag and placed it on the only chair in the "room," then showed me where the bathroom was and gave me clean towels. He explained the hot water mechanism in the bathroom and offered a general explanation of the family's schedule.

I returned to my "room," and he drew the curtain as I contemplated my situation. I planned to be in Majorca only two nights, giving myself nearly three days for exploration. The house was in a pleasant neighborhood and felt like a safe family home. And the price was cheap. I decided to stay, even though my "room" was not what I had expected. My "room" was the curtained-off end of the home's combination living and dining room!

The "Y" (YMCA or YWCA)

• You needn't be young, male or Christian to take advantage of this institution, with branches in most cities. Look for the name of the city in your "Y" catalog—or, if you haven't obtained one, do so now. Write to: The Y's Way, 224 East 47th Street, New York, NY 10017. In Hong Kong (Kowloon), I have stayed at the grand (and expensive) Peninsula Hotel *and* the YMCA across the street. I enjoyed them both.

• Send a check or money order for the first night's stay, along with your request for a reservation for your entire stay. If you don't like the accommodations, you can change to another place after the first night, though the change will use up some of your valuable travel time.

• You may be able to call and reserve a room with your credit card. You will be charged if you do not show up and do not cancel at least twenty-four hours before your reservation date.

• The Y's rooms are sometimes small and old, though others are new and modern. An inexpensive cafe is often located in the building, as well as a swimming pool and exercise room. A few YMCAs are in seedy parts of town, but the security inside is good.

Youth Hostels

In the United States I choose youth hostels when available. I've stayed in hostels in Washington, D.C., New York City, New Orleans, San Francisco, Portland, Palm Beach, Fort Lauderdale, Orlando, Key West and Cape Cod. I haven't traveled in Europe since I discovered youth hostels, but there are many more there than in the United States. The American Youth Hostel will make European reservations for you.

Here are some of the characteristics of a hostel. The buildings vary widely—from a city or country regular residence, to a historical building, to a lighthouse, to a cabin, to a 500-bed hotel. All have one or more single-sex dormitories, each with two to ten bunk beds. (Ask for a lower bunk if one is available.) Shared single-sex bathrooms provide hot-water showers and the other amenities.

A pillow and a blanket are furnished. A sheet sleep-sack can be rented, or you can bring your own. The annual membership fee is low, especially for seniors over sixty-two, and membership gives you priority for vacancies in the United States and abroad; non-members pay only a slightly higher nightly fee. The fees vary from about $12 to $20 a night.

In addition to a secure, inexpensive, clean place to sleep, there are many other advantages. Your roommates are often young, friendly women from around the world who are happy to share travel advice with you. A bulletin board or office will help you with tourist tips and information about local and long-distance transportation.

There is a shared kitchen if you want to prepare your meals, a dining area (often an outside garden) and a reading room. In addition to cleaning up after yourself, you are assigned an easy maintenance chore.

For domestic travel, look in your American Youth Hostel (AYH) booklet for the state and city you plan to visit. Occasionally a hostel is available during the summer only. If there is a hostel listed for the city or state of your choice, the rate per night will be given as well as the address and directions for reaching the hostel.

Send a check or money order for the first night's rent along with your request for a reservation for the number of nights you wish to stay. During a busy season there may be a limit to the number of nights; such limitations will be stated in the handbook listing.

If you're apprehensive about using a hostel, stay overnight in an AYH hostel close to home to learn the ropes.

SLEEP SACK ENCOUNTER

I was concentrating on a French tape coming through my earphones and for some time didn't register what my eyes were watching. Eventually I became aware of the woman struggling at the other end of the room. She was in a mighty battle trying to stuff her bunk mattress into the "mattress cover." Clearly it was her first time in a youth hostel. That morning she had met two women on a tour, and they told her they were staying here. She was delighted to move out of her dingy "cheap" motel, where she didn't feel comfortable or safe, and come to the hostel these women had praised so highly. Now she wasn't so sure about staying in a room with eight double bunks full of strangers.

Before I could separate myself from my French lessons and help her, her two newfound friends came into the room and quickly came to her aid. They began by undoing all her hard work, pulling the mattress out of its "cover."

"No, that's not for the mattress. The sack is for you. You sleep in it like a sleeping bag." The "sleep sack" had been rented at the reception desk.

The poor woman, still looking a bit dazed, smiled as her helpers spread the sack out on top of the mattress and showed her how to slip the pillow into the pocket on the underside, then tied the sack to the four posts of the bunk to stabilize it. One of the women spread the blanket on top of the sack, turned back the top of the sack and said, "Now it's ready for you to climb into when you go to bed."

"Oh, how can I thank you enough? I feel so help-less and confused. You know this is my first real *trip by myself."*

The other woman now spoke up, "I know what you mean. I can remember my first trip after my husband died. I wasn't sure I could do it, but I learned to ask for help when I needed it and found someone was always there. I don't need much help anymore.

"Come on, now. Let's go try out that Chinese restaurant down the street. I hope they have dim sum."

I smiled and returned to my French lesson.

Camping

If you love the wonders of nature, camping is the way to go. If you've forgotten the wonders of nature, camping will bring back the awesome discoveries of childhood. It may be the best way to really feel the power and glory of Mother Nature. Sleeping under the stars will awaken in you the mystery of the universe and your connection to it. Experience the day as it is born in the east, as it grows to fullness and then slips away, leaving the night to thrill you with its own delights.

I will discuss three camping methods: (1) car camping in your own car, (2) car camping with a rented car, after you have flown cross-country to your chosen destination and (3) camper camping in some form of van or pickup made for camping.

I will not discuss backpack camping here, since it's not a good way to travel alone. I'm told by my friends that backpacking is the best way to connect with our planet. There are excellent books and clubs to help you get started. On some tours you can even have your pack carried. On others, you can learn how to camp in the woods. Best of all, talk to a friend who's had experience backpack camping.

Car Camping in Your Own Car

I choose to be as comfortable as possible with a minimum of equipment. I cook very little. If you have friends with camping equipment, borrow some items until you find out how you want to camp and what *you* value in camping equipment.

Here is my basic equipment list:

• *Car bed.* If you're short enough and can make a comfortable bed in your car, do that. You'll have much more freedom in how you travel, for stopping when and where you want to, for a nap or for overnight. I met one woman driving in Mexico who had made a bed frame in the back of her Pinto. She slept on top, and the baggage went underneath.

• *A pop-up dome tent.* This doesn't have to be as lightweight or finely made as a backpack tent. I bought a simple, cheap one for about $30 at a discount house. Dome tents are free-standing and do not need to be tied down, so they can be set up on any terrain. They're awkward to set up, but once you get the knack, I think you'll like it.

- *A pad to sleep on.* I like a self-inflating foam-core type.
- *A sleeping bag.* My choice is a synthetic-filled bag of about four pounds, too heavy to use on a backpack trip, but (at about $30) not as expensive as down. Opened flat, the sleeping bag makes a good, lightweight comforter. You'll also need a bag or pillowcase to stuff with your jacket—or take along your favorite pillow.
- *A good flashlight.* Be sure to take an extra battery.
- *A hanging candle* is nice for atmospheric lighting in the tent.
- *A plastic bowl* with a tight lid is handy when nature calls.
- *An immersion heating element* or a cup with a built in immersion heater. I carry an element to plug into the cigarette lighter for heating water. You can find the cup at a motor home or camping supply store. With one of these heaters, I have hot coffee or tea any time I'm in the mood.
- *Ice chest.* I like a middle-size one that allows a carton of milk to stand up straight. You probably already have an ice chest, so don't buy a new one yet. If you choose to invest in an expensive ice chest, look into the electric ones that plug into a 12-volt plug

(with a converter you can use regular household current). The electric chest can be used with ice also.

• *Water.* Always carry a supply of safe water with you. The size of the container depends on how long you expect to be away from a source of safe water. *Do not use stream water unless you treat it by boiling for three minutes* or use another type of purification method.

• *Food.* I cook very little and depend on dry cereal with milk and *small* cans of tuna, vegetables and fruit. Often I buy prepared food, such as roast chicken and salads, from the deli section of grocery stores or specialty shops.

• *Optional items.* I most often camp in state and national parks. Some have electrical hookups and some do not. All private campgrounds, such as KOA, provide electricity and water. I have an "electric kitchen" packed in a used hard-sided suitcase. It contains an electric skillet, egg poacher, toaster and electric teapot—all of which were purchased at garage sales or at Goodwill. I only take the suitcase if I know I'll be camping where electricity is available and if I'm driving my own car. There are many fine lightweight and convenient propane camp stoves and nesting cooking pans if you want to do more cooking away from electricity.

CHEVELLE MOTEL

I stepped out into the bright, clean air on the Sea of Cortez, stretched and walked around my van. There was a new neighbor in the next camping space, a long, beat-up American sedan covered with a nylon "portable garage." Instantly I knew that I'd come upon an ingenious camping method—a way to make a private, dry tent out of my car. For years I'd been trying to figure out how to camp efficiently when I flew to a destination, rented a car and wanted to go camping. I don't like lugging a tent along with my other baggage, and sometimes I don't want to sleep in a strange campground. I remembered, one rainy night in the Everglades National Park, waking up with my tent standing in eight inches of water! Now I had a solution.

A zipper swished open and out stepped a young man who started to roll up the nylon cover. "What a great idea you have," I said, smiling my joy and appreciation.

"It's Ron's idea," he replied. I heard a sleepy groan as a skinny arm reached through the open backseat window. A pale young man with stringy blond hair rolled onto his side, grinning.

"The Los Angeles police gave me the idea. You know, sometimes I go partying and get drunk. It's against the law to sleep in your car, and it's against the law to drive drunk. What's a fellow to do? I call this the Chevelle Motel. They don't ever lift the cover to see if anyone is inside, so I just sleep it off and drive home safely in the morning."

They drove away after a few days, and while I can't be sure that car made it back home, I know they *will last forever in my memory*—especially each time I check into my own Chevelle Motel.

Camping in a Rented Car

When you've flown cross-country and want to camp, but are without your car and your usual camping gear, the easy answer is a "Chevelle Motel" (see above), using a nylon automobile cover and a rented car. I made a cover with elastic around the edge for a sedan car. For three weeks I slept in the reclining seat of my rented car and enjoyed the wonders of Newfoundland. However, if I do choose to take a tent, here is what I take:

• In a lightweight nylon duffel bag I carry the following items: tent (or car cover), sleeping bag, sleeping pad, flashlight, cigarette-lighter immersion heater, drinking cup and a plastic "night bowl." I also carry mosquito repellent and a mosquito coil. I check this bag through on my flight.

• For food I take a small can of tuna, dry cereal, sugar, a large cup, spoon and a Swiss Army knife. Before leaving the airport, or later on the way, I buy a small milk, fruit, crackers and whatever else strikes my fancy for "emergency" snacks. I do no cooking except for hot drinks. I plan to eat a good meal out once a day.

Using this method I have flown from the West Coast and camped in Maine and Florida. I experienced Everglades National Park, a state park in the Florida Keys and Acadia National Park in Maine, as well as camping in southeastern Canada.

Camper Camping

This is the easiest of all. All the conveniences and comforts of home—wherever you may roam. Next time you buy a new car, think camper van. It's so easy to stop and sleep overnight, or just take a nap in a well-lighted rest stop, hospital parking lot or anywhere there's light and other people nearby. *Do not* park alone in any deserted area, no matter how pretty it is.

Camping is not as cheap as it once was, but it is still a thrilling bargain.

Camping Information Sources

• Write for a list of state parks from the state's Parks and Recreation Department or Tourist Information Office. Write to the National Park Service for a listing of its campgrounds. All state and national parks do not have campground facilities; some are for day use only. The National Forest Service also has campgrounds with limited facilities, but often in very beautiful sites.

• Your local AAA office can provide a book listing campgrounds, public and private, as well as a tour book for each state, as well as Mexico and Canada.

• KOA offers a booklet listing all of its campgrounds. This booklet is available at any KOA campground, or you may call 1-800-548-7063 to order it.

Reservations may be required by campgrounds during peak season or when special events are scheduled nearby.

RV Travel

I've learned a lot about recreational-vehicle travel and motor-home living—and have had to give up a few preconceptions. RV owners come in all sizes, shapes, ages, genders and colors, and each has a different reason for living or traveling in a motor home.

In 1990, when I decided to step up from my beloved VW camper, I went to an RV show to see what was available. I had determined that 21 feet would meet my needs and that an expanded van would not give me anything I didn't already have.

After that, I started looking at used motor homes and eventually found a 25-foot class C (with over-the-cab bed) for only $8,000. The arrangement was excellent for me, and even though it was fourteen years old, inside and out suggested a well-cared-for vehicle.

Once I had paid for it, I panicked. The only way to deal with my fears, I knew, was to just carry on—go through the experience of driving it more than a thousand miles and living a winter in southern California as planned.

Wet, icy, cold winter arrived early, before I was ready to leave. In a lull between storms, I pulled away from home. The first ten miles would be the worst. The 4,500-foot elevation of Siskiyou Pass in southern Oregon was my first hurdle. When my friend Jim asked if I'd like him to drive me over the icy mountain pass, I answered "yes" before he could change his mind. What a gift! Once we were safely on the other side, he joined his wife in their following car.

I waved good-bye, gritted my teeth and—very carefully—drove away. Not until the third day was I confident enough about my highway driving to turn on the radio. After I got used to it, this big rig with power everything was actually easier to drive than my VW camper. All I had to do was keep it in the lane, an easy task with good sideview mirrors. After two overnight stops, I steered into the Los Angeles freeway system.

I moved right along, as if I were used to being a truck driver. As the light of day began to fade, I pulled into a highway rest stop to spend the night. I was only a few miles from my destination, Palm Springs.

In the early hours of morning, the wind began to blow. The roaring, shaking power of the wind increased as the sun climbed higher in the sky. I had not anticipated such high winds. I was driving such a big box, I decided to wait for the wind to subside. Other people drove out, but I noticed the man next to me had not budged. When I saw him out checking his trailer and pickup, I decided to consult with him about driving in the wind.

His first question was, "Where are you headed?"

"Palm Springs," I told him.

"Oh, that's no problem. It won't even be blowing as soon as you get off this road and into the valley."

"I know it's only about six miles until I turn off, but this wind is terrible." I braced myself against the truck door.

"It's always like this up here. I don't think you'll have any trouble. Me, I'm going to the Texas-Mexico border to sign on as the mechanic for a motor-home caravan to Guatemala. I'll have some slow driving across the desert."

With dry mouth and tense muscles, I pulled out into the traffic. Just over the hill was a colossal wind-mill-generated electricity farm. I guess it really does blow there often!

There was no wind at all in Palm Springs. I settled into an RV park with a splendid swimming pool and an extremely helpful staff. I explained that I had never "hooked up." The manager showed me what needed to be done. I chose not to have cable TV or a telephone, even though both were available for a modest fee.

My neighbors were a mixed-age group and had a variety of reasons for being there. There were other "snowbirds" like me, fleeing a cold winter. There were a couple of young families who either "home-schooled" their children or enrolled them in a local school. The parents had skills that permitted them to work anywhere, and they wanted their children to have a broad experience of our country.

Single women are still a minority of RV owners, but a growing number find the freedom of travel and the comfort of their home-on-wheels a perfect combination. There are even RV clubs such as RVing Women, a support network for women RVers.

Cruise or Resort Hotel

Cruise ships and resort hotels are not very useful for learning about the people and cultures of the world. However, they are often the choice of women just beginning to travel alone. I am therefore including some information.

• These are the easiest travel experiences to arrange. Your travel agent will do all the work for you, except deciding which one to choose. If you have more money than time, a cruise or resort hotel may be a wise choice. But again, you won't learn much about the places you're passing by. Sometimes a tour can be arranged through the hotel staff or cruise-ship entertainment personnel.

• For the most part, resorts and cruises are excellent if you wish to experience being pampered—for a price.

• Special off-season rates or last-minute bookings for a cruise may be very good buys. Your food, sleeping quarters and sometimes airfare are all included in the cost. Tipping and excursions are extra. You usually pay in advance, so you know *exactly* what your costs will be. Your travel agent can help you estimate tips, as well as the cost of "extra" excursions.

• *Be aware of an extra charge for a single person on a cruise.* There may be no way to avoid this extra charge, but some travel agents can get the extra charge waived or find another single passenger to share your room. There are also organizations that provide roommate-matching services.

Tips on Choosing a Cruise

If you haven't found your special travel agent, do it now. However, you still have to do your homework. How much do you want to spend? How long do you want to sail? Where do you want to go?

You are the only person who can answer those questions. After you decide, you may want to deal directly with the cruise company, a travel agent who specializes in cruises or your own agent.

Your weekly trips to the library will alert you to the many cruise specials being advertised. Another way to get information is to ask a friend who has been on cruises, where did she go? What was the name of her ship? Cruise line? Would she do that cruise again? Where will she go on her next cruise? What company? What ship?

Prices vary from an occasional bargain $100 a day to $1000 a day and more. Booking your cruise early or risking last-minute vacancies will both give you large discounts, anywhere from 10 to 50 percent.

Check on the difference in prices between a cruise that includes round-trip airfare and a cruise that doesn't. Sometimes you can make a better schedule *and* at a cheaper price if you book your own air tickets. This is most often true if you are eligible for a reduced senior fare or have "mileage plus" certificates.

Cruise lines often book your return flight home in the afternoon, even though you must disembark in the morning. So before you leave home, find out your return air schedule and see if there's an earlier flight. You can check your luggage at the cruise-ship dock if you wish, then go directly to the airport and see if you can get on an earlier flight. Your baggage will arrive later, as scheduled, but you will arrive home earlier.

Ask your travel agent about group discounts, half-price fares for second passengers and even "free" second-person fares. Then have your agent see if she can find another passenger to share the expense with you.

Be aware of "single supplements," where the single passenger pays a much higher fare (though you will, at least, have the cabin to yourself).

You will pay all your *major* expenses before you leave—your cabin and more fine food than you can ever eat. There will be other expenses. Port charges, drinks on board (even soft drinks), shore excursions and tipping of the shipboard crew are items *not* included in the cruise price.

However, you can control most of these costs. For example, a few passengers may want to rent a car to explore the country visited, for less money than the scheduled shore trip. Just be honest with yourself and your fellow companions about what you wish to afford and what you choose not to afford.

It is possible to never leave the ship and still have a splendid trip. A cruise ship is like a fine resort, with planned activities, a library, a bridge club, night clubs and a wonderfully relaxing environment where it's okay to *just do nothing*.

Your ship may stop at a different port every day or only two or three over the whole cruise. There are advantages to both ways, but as on any other trip, don't wear yourself out by greedily trying to do and see it "all." *You can't*. Be selective and savor each taste, smell, sound and touch along the way.

I prefer a mix of passenger ages, from toddlers to elegant elders. The longer and more expensive the cruise, the older the passengers tend to be. There are also special cruises for singles, bridge clubs, health improvement, spa cruises, adventure, gambling…The cruising world has something for everyone.

Do not expect large hotel-style rooms. Most cabins are smaller than you expect. Cheaper cabins are on the lower decks and on the inside without a porthole. However, they are comfortable and adequate for sleeping. That is all you will do there. For reading, writing, sipping tea, people-watching and promenading, there are plenty of other rooms and plenty of space on deck.

If you're afraid you'll get seasick, talk to your doctor. There are many choices of anti-seasickness pills and patches. On many of the large stabilized cruise ships, you're barely able to detect any movement on deck. It's unlikely you'll experience discomfort.

WHAT WILL YOU EAT?

Like Napoleon's army, a traveler travels on her stomach. Don't neglect your nutrition—don't fast and don't overload your digestive system. Do have *fun* eating.

Tasting was the first way we explored our strange new world when we were born. It is still an excellent way to explore any strange new world or culture. Often I see something on the menu or in the market that I've never tasted—*that's* what I order.

Suggestions for Choosing Restaurants

• Walk outside your hostel or hotel and walk around in the neighborhood. See what eating places are available. Are any of them busy during meal hours? Do the patrons look like local people, or tourists? (Go with what draws the locals.)

• Check the menus displayed in the windows of several cafes. If you're traveling abroad, is the menu in English or in the local language?

• Is there a "fixed price" meal?" This can be your best bet.

• Do they serve breakfast? Lunch? Dinner? Is there a take-out menu?

• Do the prices fit your budget? Check your currency-exchange table carefully.

In addition to what you may find near your hotel, I hope you've already chosen some restaurants based on your pretravel research. If you've always wanted to eat at Maxim's in Chicago or Paris, *do it*. And dress the part—that's why you brought those beautiful scarves. But don't go on your first night in town. Save the experience for when you're rested and relaxed.

Other tips:

• Eat a large lunch or a large late breakfast (after tea/coffee/fruit in your room earlier). These meals are cheaper than dinner and give you fuel for afternoon activities.

• Shop for picnic food in grocery stores, delicatessens, open markets, bakeries, roadside stands, drug stores—anywhere the local people shop. Don't get stuck with an old prejudice about what *should* be eaten for breakfast or any meal. Think in terms of what your body needs to eat in a day. I often eat tuna for breakfast for a good protein starter, and I eat cereal *any* time of day. Europeans eat fish for breakfast as well as cheese. Be sure you eat enough bulk and drink sufficient safe liquids. You're probably walking more than usual and need more calories. Go easy on the alcohol and chocolate.

• Picnic for breakfast and dinner—in your room, in a park, on the road such as the English do, in cathedral or museum gardens, on trains and buses, wherever there is space and time.

• Always carry a small bottle of safe water to drink.

• Remember to take your immersion heater, large plastic cup, tea, instant coffee, sugar, spoon, Swiss Army knife and can/bottle opener.

Careful Eating Makes for a Good Trip

"Boil it, cook it, peel it or forget it!"
—United States Centers for Disease Control

I am *very* careful about what I eat during my travels. I find out before I leave if the water is safe to drink. The United States Centers for Disease Control can tell you this. If I have *any* doubts about the water I become supercautious. I drink only sealed bottled water and eat *no salads or other uncooked vegetables.* Be sure to wash your teeth and toothbrush in bottled water or even Coca Cola, not tap water, and use *no ice* in your drinks (unless you *know* it is made from bottled water). Alcoholic drinks do not sterilize the ice water. I end up drinking much more cold beer than usual when I travel.

"Boil it, cook it, peel it or forget it!" is the best advice I know. However, this doesn't mean you can't try new foods, eat well and have a good trip.

• Cooked foods must be hot. Eat meals at the same time the natives do, so the food will be freshly cooked. For example, in Guatemala the little store next to my hotel made delicious tamales on Sunday afternoon. I ate them with delight. The tamales prepared on Sunday might still be available on Monday or Tuesday, but I would never eat them then. Find out when the food was cooked, by asking *and* observing.

As for freshly made "street food," the danger comes from being served in a just-washed and wet plate or glass. Provide your own plate, cup or container so there's no contaminated water on the serving container. The taste of fresh-fried, grilled or baked local food, eaten outside a temple or sitting under a swaying palm tree, may be one of your fondest memories. Tea and coffee are usually safe.

• Fresh fruit from an exotic open-air market can be safe and delightful if you follow my suggestions. I take with me or buy locally *tincture of iodine.* Almost any pharmacy will have it, although buying locally means you have to find out the word for iodine in the local language.

I buy fruit that's easily peeled (no berries, grapes etc.), then take the melon, mango, papaya, oranges or whatever back to my room and run the sink full of water. I put about 20 to 40 drops of iodine in the water and soak the fruit in the iodine water for at least an hour, then peel it and enjoy. Bananas are the only fruit I eat without soaking. Even then, be sure to keep your own hands off the banana pulp while peeling.

• You'll probably end up eating a high meat and carbohydrate diet following these rules against eating uncooked vegetables. For constipation I bring along Metamucil to provide bulk, taking a large teaspoonful each day if needed.

• Even with all precautions, the change in foods and water, the stress and exertions accompanying travel may lead to an upset digestive system. I take Pepto-Bismol (available in most pharmacies), drink lots of water or other fluids and rest. I always have one or two tablets of Lomotil or Imodine from my own physician to stop stools for a short time on a long bus ride or other inconvenient place. These do nothing to cure the upset; they just stop the action for a short while.

Kabobs in Kabul

Years ago, I settled into a comfortable room in the most expensive hotel in Kabul, Afghanistan. From my balcony I could see a small food shop across the dirt street. My mouth began to drool as the tantalizing aroma of skewered meat roasting on an open fire wafted my way.

I didn't want to go and eat there, nor eat on plates newly rinsed with polluted water. What was I to do? I had to have some of that meat! The only container I could find was an empty candy tin with a few hard candies left inside. I dropped the candy on the dresser and off I went, following an aromatic trail.

I held up five fingers, pointed to the shish kabobs and held out the tin. The vendor smiled and, using his hot fork, pushed the tidbits of lamb off the metal skewers into the tin. I could hardly wait to get back to my room for the feast.

MEETING MEN ALONG THE WAY

There are so many "rules" for women in the diverse cultures of the world that you can't possibly know them all. However, here are some general notes on that subject.

American movies are seen and *believed* all over the world. Therefore, all men "know" that American women are "easy." It is a fact of travel that you will have to deal with in your own way. I use conservative clothes and do not look men in the eyes. Often eye contact is seen as an invitation or dare. Be purposeful in your walk and posture. Never show signs of helplessness or weakness.

This does not mean you cannot ask for help. Most people, men included, are generous with their assistance when asked directly. I usually ask a man who has a woman with him, or a well-dressed older man in a busy open space—train station, street corner, etc.

Several young women have told me they wear wedding rings when traveling, but that they need to look like real ones, not cheap imitations. Still, I remove my wedding ring when I travel—first, because it's valuable and I never wear or carry valuable items when I travel, and second, because I find that I'm treated more as an individual and have more interesting conversations without my wedding ring.

FRIENDLY INVITATIONS

Some women find the "man of their dreams" while traveling, although dreaming of men is the last thing I want to do when I'm on the road. Even so, I've had some interesting encounters.

One encounter took place in the Geneva, Switzerland, train station. I had a three-hour wait before my overnight train to Munich.

A pleasant-looking man, short and a little plump, like me, said "Good evening" and tipped his hat. "Is your train late?"

My book wasn't very interesting, so I wasn't annoyed by his interruption. "No, I think it will be on time."

"Why don't you come have supper with me? We could talk and...you know, enjoy each other."

Probably a faint smile slipped across my face before I put on my stern facade. "No, thanks," I said. "I've had supper." I returned to my reading. He didn't go away.

We talked of many things, but mostly about his village in Italy and his family. He asked about my husband and children, and explained how lonely it was to have to work in a foreign land, away from those he loved.

After one final invitation ("You're sure you won't have dinner with me?"), he tipped his hat again and walked away.

While traveling in Maine, I learned about men who hang out at the hotel check-in counter. The phone in my room at the Bangor Hilton rang around eight at night.

"Hello, Jay? This is Fred. I was wondering if I could bring some food over to your room. We could have a light supper together."

"How did you get my room number?" I was shocked, a little frightened—and curious. "Where are you?"

He replied, "Oh, I'm in room 506. Would you rather come to my room?"

He sounded so friendly, at ease and straightforward. My curiosity got the best of me. "How about coffee downstairs. I've already eaten," I lied.

After a long pause, he finally responded, "Well, okay. See you downstairs."

"How will I know you?"

"Oh, don't worry. I know what you look like."

We talked for a couple of hours. He was a handsome blond traveling jewelry salesman, surprised when I knew the name of the gold ankh he wore on a gold chain about his neck. He was the first and only Rosicrucian I've ever met, and was willing to talk about it.

When I asked how he had learned my name and room number, he explained that his habit was to hang out at the check-in counter of his hotel. When he saw a woman who looked pleasant and wholesome, or dignified, or interesting in some other way, he would listen for the number of her room and look at the name tag on her luggage.

I was impressed—but not impressed enough to invite him to my room. I did carefully double-lock my room and drape the security chain in place across my door.

Another time, when I was in the Middle East, a talkative taxi driver wildly wended his way from the Beirut airport to what was then a glistening city, the Pearl of the Middle East. Set on the blue Mediterranean, Beirut's ancient arched stone remnants nestled close to glittering glass buildings, with Jaguars, Ferraris, and long, black Lincoln Continentals swarming about like little ants.

By the time we reached my hotel the taxi driver had offered to be my guide, confidant and more. I laughingly said, "No, thank you, I'll be fine." I *handed him the money for the fare, and he thanked me. Then with a twinkle in his eyes and a courtly flourish of his arm he gave me his card.*

"In case you change your mind, I'm available at this number."

TRAVELING WITH A CHILD

There is no comparison between traveling as a family and traveling one-to-one with a child. It is a rare opportunity we seldom give ourselves. Two of my favorite memories are traveling with my thirteen-year-old son and, years later, traveling with my grandson when he was thirteen.

I like the age thirteen or fourteen. As my son explained, "I'm still young enough to not be embarrassed to ask questions, and old enough to remember the answers." At this age, children are used to teachers and pay close attention to docents or tour leaders as the points of interest are explained. Of course, they're not always interested in what *you* want them to like. My son remembers the man shouting, *"Caffè Caldo"* at intermission much more clearly than he remembers the opera *Aida* at the Caracalla Baths in Rome. I remember *my fear* as he sat on the edge of the Estrella fountain, at night, watching the mad cars race by this busy intersection in Rome.

I *should* have been afraid when he climbed the Great Pyramid of Giza—in his rubber thong sandals. Our first view of the hazy moonlit shadow of the Great Pyramid looming high outside our Mena House hotel room is one we will never forget. The climb to the top is no longer allowed because of the danger, but the view is still there for each new traveler.

More recently, I have memories of discovering that my grandson is a virtuoso with people, with an easy, immediate ability to relate to shopkeepers, travelers, airline personnel and anyone else he chooses. For example, I was surprised and delighted to see him working as a "go-for" at an international conference I attended in India. He soon knew how to move about the Oberoi Hotel in Bombay, dealing with caterers and convention managers, as well as the front desk personnel. I treasure my photograph of him at the Colosseum in Rome and at the Jefferson Monument in Washington, D.C.

Once you have become an experienced solo traveler, *I highly recommend traveling with one young teenager you love.* "One" is the key word in that sentence.

Traveling with a young adult has its own special rewards. Travel with my daughter in Mexico and along the Oregon coast, away from the demands of work and family, was priceless. We renewed old connections and made new ones. Best of all was a trip we made to Georgia, where together we found our roots—and scores of new memories.

OTHER TRAVEL OPTIONS

Service/Travel

"Are you an old-fashioned nurse?" Sister Maria's voice was strong and friendly as it came through the telephone.

"Yes, I am." My reply was somewhat tentative, as I hadn't taught nursing in many years. I was sure that I could be of some value to the Mexican nursing students in Zacapu.

You too can find a place to mix service and travel, no matter what your area of expertise is. Even more important, you can discover novel work in an unexplored place and begin a fascinating new life—at any age.

I started by joining an organization called Project Concern International, a clearinghouse for nonprofit organizations in the United States and around the world. Their work is to match people with organizations looking for personnel, both paid staff and volunteers. Most of the need is for medical-related personnel, but also includes secretaries, administrators, librarians and agronomists. The organization will send you a brochure if you write to P.O. Box 85323, San Diego, CA 92186. Soon after my sixty-seventh birthday I was offered a chance to work in Thailand as a volunteer. (Instead, I volunteered a few months at the nursing school in Mexico.)

If you want to live in a state or national park, it's easy. For information on the national parks, write to the specific park where you want to help or to the VIP Coordinator in the Regional Headquarters of your choice. You will receive a pamphlet "Volunteers in Parks" explaining the VIP program and including a map of all national parks and monuments. For state parks, write to the Parks and Recreation Department in the state of your choice, or to a particular state park.

You usually must furnish your own living quarters: trailer, motor home or tent. The park furnishes free hookups, or at least electricity. Occasionally, the park is able to provide housing. So if you yearn to spend a month or a season at the beach, the mountains or at a historical monument, they need you out there.

Your church or synagogue is another place to inquire about volunteering at overseas missions. Habitat for Humanity needs builders and office workers. The Small Business Bureau can connect you to a volunteer organization that advises small businesses and industries in developing countries. Don't forget that the Peace Corps and VISTA are still busy helping out at home and abroad.

In your local library you'll find a number of helpful books, such as *Volunteer Vacations, Working in Paradise* and *Helping Out Outdoors.* Once you start looking, you'll be amazed at the choices. *So start looking now.*

Work/Travel

I have not had the experience of working my way around the country or the world, but I can tell you other people's stories.

At the youth hostel in Key West, Florida, I became aware for the first time of the presence of notes on the bulletin board announcing jobs for short-term work, primarily in resort areas. The jobs were for buspersons, dishwashers, housekeepers and, occasionally, for waiters.

Years later I saw the process at work. One night a very young French woman arrived in the New Orleans youth hostel. She was dressed in black with matching very black hair, highly sophisticated yet quite friendly. In a day and a half she had found an apartment to share and a job. She planned to stay in New Orleans for at least six weeks. She tried to get a job at some of the fancy French restaurants, but was unsuccessful. She took a job selling souvenirs in the French Quarter.

The key to her success was confidence, willingness to take any job that was available and determination to take care of the "have to's" first—a place to live and a way to make money. Sightseeing would come later.

Another young woman from New Jersey came with the purpose of moving to New Orleans. No, she *had* moved. Her car was crammed full of her belongings and she knew it was a prime target for robbery. She went out the first day to look for a job. She found work in a video store because she had experience. She was ready to find a place to live.

Then there was Elizabeth. I met her working in a travel office that books places to stay in Europe. She worked there on the weekend. Back home, she had worked as a medical records secretary in a hospital. While I waited to be served she told me her story.

She explained how, when she lived in Los Angeles, she had taken stock of her situation. She wanted to drive across the country, but looked at her financial situation and realized that she couldn't possibly afford it—and never would.

A year later, she realized she had driven 4,000 miles and *never left Los Angeles*. She sold or gave away everything she could not take with her in her truck and started across the United States. She stopped where she wanted to, then found a job and stayed there as long as she wanted to—still living in her truck. She is a plain-looking past-middle-age woman. You would never notice her walking down the street. She hides her enormous courage and zest for life behind her friendly smile and dancing eyes.

After a while she grew tired of living in the truck. "It was hard to stay neat to look for work or go to work," she told me. So she started renting a room or an apartment in each town where she stopped to work. She has seen most of the United States—north, south, east and now is back in the West. I suspect her weekend work in the travel office is a prologue for living some future dream of traveling outside the United States.

As I see it, Elizabeth's secret was the willingness—and the courage—to reduce her expenses (little or no rent, no telephone or other utilities). She knew she had very saleable skills—medical-records transcribing and general secretarial. She was also willing to take whatever jobs were available to live her dream of traveling.

Finally, if you haven't seen the movie *Shirley Valentine* lately, rent it at the video store. I think every woman should see that movie at least twice a year.

Dream your dreams and live your dreams.

Personal Development Travel

Of course, all travel contributes to personal development. As I said at the beginning of this book, if you are not changed in some way by your travel, you've missed one of its main rewards. Here, however, I want to point out a path more specifically oriented toward personal development.

Esalen Institute, in Big Sur, California, was one of the first and most famous centers offering retreats for the spirit-mind-body, and it is still going strong. Since then, there are practically unlimited numbers and types of personal growth centers in the United States and around the world.

Just decide what you're looking for—meditation, massage, weight loss, stop smoking, psychotherapy, tai chi, dance—somewhere there is a weekend, week-long or longer program just for you. To find out where, ask someone you know involved in the process in which you are interested. Ask your librarian, your doctor and, of course, your travel agent.

You may want to have a silent (or nearly so) retreat on your own. Camping in the woods can provide that, but ask your minister or rabbi if he or she knows of such a retreat center. Many churches have large camp or ranch retreat facilities for adults of any denomination. The Presbyterian Ghost Ranch in New Mexico is one fine example. The Seventh Day Adventists have a large number of health spas across the country. Check with the churches and synagogues in your town.

Educational Travel

> *"Learning something totally new is like going from a windowless room out onto a bright balcony and discovering a whole new universe spread before you."*
>
> *—Carter Croley, world traveler, by bicycle, sailboat and on foot*

Many colleges and universities offer programs that take paying volunteers to help on archeological digs, band birds for the study of their flight patterns, rebuild ancient stone houses in France and Italy, etc.

Elderhostel is the major source for educational and adventure trips for people over the age of sixty. Each year they add new countries and new studies, although their programs are so popular that you still may not get your first choice.

Many colleges have started their own "elder adventures" or "learning in retirement" programs. (Your local college may provide just what you're looking for.) They often combine travel with a writing or painting workshop, intensive foreign-language course, introduction to computers or update on new software, woodworking, bronze casting…the list is limited only by your imagination.

It's easy for a single person to join these tour groups, even though you may have to pay a single supplement.

If you are willing to share a room, be sure to ask for a roommate assignment.

Adventure Travel

Frommer's book, *A New World of Travel,* is an excellent place to start researching this area. Several companies specialize in women-only tours or activities. Whether you want to learn to rock-climb, kayak, white-water raft through the Grand Canyon, trek in

Nepal or investigate the politics of a foreign country, someone is available to take you there.

RANDOM TIPS

Maps: On my recent trip to New York I cut Manhattan out of a larger map of metropolitan New York. I knew I was only going to visit Manhattan. I took that section of the map and enlarged it on a copy machine so that I could read the street names easily. I marked the site of my hostel in bright red so I never had to search for it again. That way, I could easily orient myself.

Paper and books: These are heavy. It is a constant battle between what I want to take or acquire along the way and the increasing weight of those acquisitions (brochures, books, articles, free flight magazines, etc.). Here are a few tricks.

I was given a heavy hardback book just before I left home. I wanted to read it, but did not want to carry it, so I mailed it to my final destination, the home of a friend, and was able to read it and carry it only during the last leg of my trip. Hotels and hostels will hold mail for you too.

When I'm on an extended trip and want to gather information for my writing or to share with friends, I take along heavy manila envelopes and mail the collected paper brochures, postcards, etc., to my home address. Sometimes the postage is high, but it's better than carrying the extra weight. If you forget to take envelopes, you can nearly always find them locally.

Local events at your destination: In cities that have an English-language newspaper, buy one. Examine it carefully for events such as craft shows, lectures, workshops, performances and demonstrations. You may find something of special interest to you *and* another opportunity to mix with the local people and sample a bit of their life. During a recent stay in Albuquerque I went to a Southwestern Writers Workshop, a travel exhibit, an annual art festival and a lecture by a famous environmentalist. I had found them listed in the calendar of events in the local newspaper.

Bulletin boards at youth hostels and laundromats are also sources of information about local events.

EPILOGUE

Putting It All Together—My Trip to New York City

"The real question is: What is your life worth and what are you going to do with it?"
—*David Viscott, M.D., in* Feel Free

The Matisse retrospective exhibit at the Museum of Modern Art and a special low fare on Amtrak trains catapulted me into a frenzy of excitement and research. I had never visited New York on my own—and never before wanted to. Now I could hardly wait. I chose my dates and made my train reservation to cross this broad continent on a route just below the Canadian border. I'd see the wide expanse of the northern states—Washington, Idaho, Montana, Wyoming, North Dakota—as well as metropolitan cities in Minnesota, Illinois and New York.

The library became my second home as I read the Sunday *New York Times* for current and near-future happenings—concerts, exhibits, operas and plays. *New Yorker* magazine gave an even more extensive listing, and I decided to buy the current issue as soon as I arrived in New York. I checked out several guidebooks and went to the AAA for maps and another guidebook.

Before I settled down to read my guidebooks, I called a local American Youth Hostel (AYH) to get the telephone number and address of the New York City hostel. Even though I had a friend in New York who would let me stay with her and her husband, I wanted to stay where I was totally on my own. I would plan one special evening together with these generous and busy people.

I called the New York International Youth Hostel to make a reservation and was told that since I was coming at a slow tourist time, October, I would not need a reservation.

With my room settled, I concentrated on making a priority list of activities for my six days in the Big Apple.

I arrived at four on a weekday afternoon at Penn Station. It was not nearly as crowded as I expected, since I had arrived before the rush hour. With my bags firmly attached to a luggage cart I explored the station, bought a current *New Yorker* and made my way to the street. To my great delight and surprise I saw a taxi booth on the corner. I had come to expect them at airports and bus stations in Mexico, but in New York? I told the booth attendant the address of my hostel, and he chose a taxi, lifted my bags and cart into the trunk, and closed the door behind me. I repeated the address to the driver.

The hostel is a huge, well-marked building covering nearly a whole block. Inside is a large, rather bare lobby with a registration desk at one end and a security desk at the other. A courteous young woman checked me in, and I carried my luggage to the second floor via the elevator. I had asked for a lower bunk and was lucky to get the last one in a five-double-bunk dormitory. A clean bathroom with showers was down a long, well-lighted hall. With some exploration I found in the basement a communal kitchen, a dining room, and stairs leading to a lovely large outdoor garden with tables and chairs. On the first floor was a cozy reading room and an information desk with bus schedules, activities, etc. There was also a message board.

Each time I went in and out of the lobby, I had to show my room receipt and room keycard. A nuisance, but also reassuring.

Next I explored the mildly seedy neighborhood in the dusky light. I found a small Spanish restaurant across the street and ordered a huge bowl of ham-hock stew. Tasty, filling, cheap—and only $2.

Day One: Matisse Exhibit and New York Public Library

My first priority was to get tickets to the Matisse retrospective at the Museum of Modern Art.

Before I left the hostel I asked questions and learned that subways are called "trains" and that buses run "uptown," "downtown" or "crosstown." The fare for trains or buses is $1.25 and you had to have correct *change* for the bus—not even a dollar bill and a quarter will do. I was pleased to learn that people over sixty-five with a Medicare card can ride both the trains and buses for half price.

I decided to risk the train and chose the rush hour as the most comfortable time for me. Holding up my Medicare card, I pushed my five quarters under the window and tried to tell the clerk I wanted two tokens. She pushed one token under the window and gave me a transfer. I thought, "Oh, well" and hurried along with the commuting crowd. "I'll try to figure out how to get my half fare another time." I waited until the next day to read my transfer. It was good for another ride on the train, any train. I had, after all, received my half-fare rate.

I took a downtown train to Lincoln Center and began to walk to the Museum of Modern Art. Of course I walked in the wrong direction at first, which meant I arrived at the museum later than I'd planned. I joined the already long line outside the museum and waited for about an hour in the nippy cool morning. There was some doubt that there would be enough tickets available for people as far back as I was in the line. Some people left but I stayed on, and I was eventually rewarded with tickets for later in the day.

My second priority was to visit the central branch of the New York Public Library at Fifth Avenue and 42nd Street. PBS had shown an inspiring film about the building and philosophy of that great institution. So, checking my map, I walked to the library, a handsome structure of white marble guarded by two great marble lions. I knew Lady Luck was with me when I discovered that a tour of the building was about to start. Led by a well-informed volunteer, I visited the French walnut-paneled periodical rooms and other special rooms before arriving in the great reading room with its original long oak tables and brass lamps. There is also a "writer's room" that any writer with a contract from a publisher may use, a map section, a Hebrew section and many other special collections. Books cannot be checked out but must be read in the library. Even with a staggering 800 shelf-miles of books in the basement of the main building, plus 400 more miles of books beneath a park next door, a book takes no more than fifteen minutes to arrive at the request desk. That great efficiency is attained using the original vacuum retrieval system.

I left this fine institution with just enough time to walk rapidly back to the museum to see the Matisse exhibit at the designated time. Oh, how wonderful to view the 400 paintings, sculptures and cutouts that represent Henri Matisse's long, productive life. I took my time, retracing my steps and lingering as long as I wished. After four hours I was exhausted, so I sat a while in the outdoor sculpture garden to rest.

This long, overfilled day ended with a lovely visit and spaghetti dinner with my friends, followed by an expensive taxi ride back to the hostel late at night.

Day Two: Lincoln Center and the Performing Arts Library

I hung out in my room and in the garden until noon, recuperating from the previous day's grand exhaustion. Then I headed back on the train to Lincoln Center. I walked about the square admiring the facades and fountains, and finally made my way to the line for tickets to a concert by the New York

Philharmonic Orchestra. There were no cheap tickets, so I decided this would be my big splurge and bought a $35 ticket to the next morning's eleven o'clock concert. I then crossed the square to stand in line for opera tickets. I couldn't get my first choice, but was able to buy a $10 ticket to *Carmen*.

Across the square again at the Performing Arts Library, I discovered a mime show in progress and watched the final act. Downstairs I found an exhibit of Italian puppets, some as large as a room, as well as every other size. Nearby the high, reedy voice of a soprano recorded on an old victrola record wafted down the hall leading me to an exhibit of a woman's clothes and other mementos (such as a melted metal purse with gold coins clinging to it) that survived the San Francisco earthquake and fire of 1906. Also displayed was a letter to the woman from the manager of the St. Francis Hotel, reporting that most of her things had been lost in the fire.

After visiting the music-listening room, where every turntable was in use, I decided to go back to the hostel since it was getting late and I was getting tired. I caught an uptown bus and got off a little too soon. This turned out to be a good move, as there were several Chinese restaurants along the street. I chose one with the unlikely name of Tokyo-Szechuan.

Inside, the restaurant lived up to its name with a sushi/sashimi bar in front, in addition to an extensive menu of Japanese and Chinese cooked dishes. I indulged in a delicious Szechuan duck dinner. With tip it came to only $10. Then I walked just a few blocks to my welcome bed.

Day Three: Concert and the Frick Collection

My day started over a large cup of very good coffee and a not-so-great pastry. I had found a bakery/coffee shop only two and a half blocks from the hostel. I ordered a refill of coffee and another pastry and carried it onto the train to Lincoln Center. There I sat on the broad black-marble side of the main fountain and sipped my coffee as I watched a group of schoolchildren touring the center with their teachers. Soon the audience began to arrive at Avery Hall for the concert, and I joined them.

Inside, I discovered my seat was ideal, near the center and about a third of the way back from the orchestra. As the concert began, my body and mind felt and heard this terrific orchestra of a hundred or so musicians playing as if they were one great instrument. I had forgotten how long it had been since I had heard great music played by a great orchestra. I swam in an ecstasy of humility, excitement, and thankfulness.

I moved slowly out of the auditorium and onto the street. After a while I was ready to make my way to a crosstown bus and my next destination.

I had only recently learned of the Frick collection from a mention in a book about small art museums. I recognized the building, located directly across Fifth Avenue from the Metropolitan Museum of Art, from pictures I'd seen. The grand mansion had once been the home of American industrialist and art collector Henry Clay Frick and family, and the collection was primarily a mixture of Gainsboroughs, Holbeins, Whistlers and a few Impressionists. After my first walk through the museum, I made a second trip, pausing to enjoy my favorite paintings and to study those that didn't attract me, hoping at least to understand them better.

Again tired but richly fed by the sounds and sights of the day, I made my way home on the train. I could hardly believe the thrilling visit I was having—alone, and a little light-headed with the freedom to choose my destinations and how I spent my time there.

Day Four: Metropolitan Museum of Art

Sleeping late and having a leisurely breakfast prepared me for my next priority, the Magritte exhibit at the Met. I've never been much of a fan of Surrealist art, but wanted to see what Magritte had to say. I wandered through a couple of rooms, and sometimes he made me laugh—a huge nose, an apparent erect penis that turned out to be a small statue of a woman, an easel painted into a window scene. (The painting on the easel was of the tree that was obscured by the painting.) Part of the exhibit was a room full of books about the paintings, so I sat and rested and read for a while. It was a pleasant and educational experience for me, leaving me with a much friendlier understanding of Surrealist painting.

Next I tried to find my way to the permanent collection of Islamic and Middle Eastern art. The Met was undergoing repairs, and I had a hard time finding my destination—but what a rewarding destination! I have seen a lot of Islamic, Middle Eastern and Indian art. The Met's fine artifacts were wonderfully woven into an extremely coherent movement from one section to another.

Hours had passed since I'd arrived at the museum and I was running down. I wanted to go rest at the Tiffany glass exhibit, but I never made it. Through the maze of construction I arrived at the museum's gift shop, where I bought some cards and Tiffany note cards. Then I headed home.

Day Five: Rest Day

I spent the entire day at the hostel, with a couple of ventures out to nearby eateries. I slept, read and wrote cards, letters and diary entries. I called home to check in and tell my family what a wonderful trip I was having. I sat in the garden in the sunshine talking to fellow travelers, then back to bed.

Day Six: Ellis Island and the Statue of Liberty

I took an early train to catch the ferry to Ellis Island and the newly established museum honoring the masses of immigrants who have passed through that port of entry. It was a humbling experience. The museum is a monument to the adaptability and indomitable spirit of human beings. Careworn faces in old photographs reminded me of all the freedoms I take for granted and the great hopes our country once held out for both old and new citizens.

I chose not to visit Liberty Island, but viewed the awesome lady from a distance.

Day Seven: Departure

I had forgotten my alarm clock and needed to get up at four the next morning, so I asked one of my roommates if I could borrow hers. She seemed a little reluctant because she needed to get up at nine. I promised to reset the alarm, so she lent it to me. My roommates were a quiet mix of young women—two very friendly Australians, a Frenchwoman (who loaned me the clock) and a stunning Japanese woman with long, super-curled hair in the latest style.

Up on time, I dressed, gathered my belongings (I had packed my bags the night before) and headed down to the checkout desk to return my rented sheets and room key. I picked up my hostel membership card and walked out into the well-lighted street. I felt very alone standing under the streetlight with so little traffic. I almost didn't notice a speeding taxi but managed to wave just as the driver was passing. He came to a quick stop and backed up to pick me up. I had waited no more than five minutes.

Once settled on the train, I leaned back in my spacious seat, blew up my travel pillow, plugged in my ear phones and listened to my tape of the New York Philharmonic Orchestra playing "Bolero" as my thrilling culture orgy came to an end.

New York, New York. Next year, Paris.

RESOURCES

Access Foundation for the
Disabled
P.O. Box 356
Malverne, NY 11565

AARP (American Associ-
ation of Retired Persons)
3200 E. Carson Street
Lakewood, CA 90712

Elderhostel
75 Federal Street
Boston, MA 02110

International Gay Travel
Association
P.O. Box 4972
Key West, FL 33041

International Youth
Hostels Association
P.O. Box 37613
Washington, D.C. 20013

KOA (Kampgrounds of
America)
Reservation Central
Call 1-800-548-7063

Mobility International
P.O. Box 3551
Eugene, OR 97403

Outdoor Vacations for
Women Over Forty
P.O. Box 200
Groton, MA 01450

Project Hope
(volunteer service travel)
People Health Foundation
Carter Hall
Millwood, VA 22646

RVing Women
201 E. Southern Avenue
Apache Junction, AZ
85219

Servas (visitor exchange)
11 John Street
New York, NY 10038

Sierra Club
730 Polk Street
San Francisco, CA 94109

Travel Companion
Exchange
P.O. Box 833
Amityville, NY 11701

Traveling Women
(publication)
855 Moraga Drive #14
Los Angeles, CA 90049

Wander Women
(publication)
136 N. Grand Avenue #237
West Covina, CA 91791

Womanship
137 Conduit Street
Annapolis, MD 21401

Womantrek
1411 E. Olive Way
P.O. Box 20643
Seattle, WA 98102

INDEX

photo by Kathy Hollis Cooper

ABOUT THE AUTHOR

Jay Ben-Lesser has traveled around the world thirteen times. Her knowledge of human behavior comes from twenty years of private practice working with women as a psychotherapist. She lives in Ashland, Oregon.

The Crossing Press
publishes a full selection
of titles of interest to women.
To receive our current catalog,
please call toll-free,

800·777·1048.